COVENANT · BIBLE · STUDIES

Mystery and Glory in John's Gospel

Dorotha Winger Fry

faithQuest
the trade imprint of Brethren Press

Covenant Bible Study Series

Mystery and Glory in John's Gospel

Dorotha Winger Fry

Cover design by Jeane Healy
Cover photo by W. Perry Conway / Tom Stack & Associates

Library of Congress Catalog Card Number: 92-54261

Manufactured in the United States of America

Contents

Foreword

The Covenant Bible Study Series was first developed for a denominational program in the Church of the Brethren and the Christian Church (Disciples of Christ). This program, called People of the Covenant, was founded on the concept of relational Bible study and has been adopted by several other denominations and small groups who want to study the Bible in a community rather than alone.

Relational Bible study is marked by certain characteristics, some of which differ from other types of Bible study. For one, it is intended for small groups of people who can meet face-to-face on a regular basis and share frankly with an intimate group.

It is important to remember that relational Bible study is anchored in covenantal history. God covenanted with people in Old Testament history, established a new covenant in Jesus Christ, and covenants with the church today.

Relational Bible study takes seriously a corporate faith. As each person contributes to study, prayer, and work, the group becomes the real body of Christ. Each one's contribution is needed and important. "For just as the body is one and has many members, and all the members of the body, though many, are one body, so it is with Christ. . . . Now you are the body of Christ and individually members of it" (1 Cor. 12:12, 17).

Relational Bible study helps both individuals and the group to claim the promise of the Spirit and the working of the Spirit. As one person testified, "In our commitment to one another and in our sharing, something happened. . . . We were woven together in love by the master Weaver. It is something that can happen only when two or three or seven are gathered in God's name, and we know the promise of God's presence in our lives."

The symbol for these covenant Bible study groups is the burlap cross. The interwoven threads, the uniqueness of each strand, the unrefined fabric, and the rough texture characterize covenant groups. The people in the groups are unique but interrelated; they are imperfect and unpolished, but loving and supportive.

The shape that these divergent threads create is the cross, the symbol for all Christians of the resurrection and presence with us of Christ our Savior. Like the burlap cross, we are brought together, simple and ordinary, to be sent out again in all directions to be in the world.

For people who choose to use this study in a small group, the following guidelines will help create an atmosphere in which support will grow and faith will deepen.

1. As a small group of learners, we gather around God's word to discern its meaning for today.
2. The words, stories, and admonitions we find in scripture come alive for today, challenging and renewing us.
3. All people are learners and all are leaders.
4. Each person will contribute to the study, sharing the meaning found in the scripture and helping to bring meaning to others.
5. We recognize each other's vulnerability as we share out of our own experience, and in sharing we learn to trust others and to be trustworthy.

Additional suggestions for study and group-building are provided in the "Sharing and Prayer" section. They are intended for use in the hour preceding the Bible study to foster intimacy in the covenant group and relate personal sharing to the Bible study topic.

Welcome to this study. As you search the scriptures, may you also search yourself. May God's voice and guidance and the love and encouragement of brothers and sisters in Christ challenge you to live more fully the abundant life God promises.

Preface

In any good mystery, the clues are hidden in the story. Devotees of mystery learn how to read the signs and think like a sleuth using obscure details to solve the puzzle before the book does. Library copies of Gardner, Christie, and Holmes stories are dog-eared from use and television productions of mysteries are winning all kinds of awards.

But for the most spectacular mystery, turn to the Gospel of John. It is full of signs and clues about the identity of Jesus. Through mysterious sayings and signs, Jesus reveals that he is the full expression of God's will sent to glorify "the Father."

While the signs and wonders are mysterious, they are hardly obscure. Jesus says outright, "I am the way," " I am the truth," "I am the door," I am the vine." He changes water to wine and performs miracles of healing. What are we to make of Jesus' mysterious claims? As we read the familiar stories in these studies, we will see that the meaning of Jesus' sayings and wonders are very obvious to the faithful and completely incomprehensible to the unbeliever.

These ten lessons focus on themes of mystery and glory in the Gospel of John. In discussions of "I am" statements, exploration of Jesus' mission, and Jesus' example to us at the last supper, we can test our vision. Do we see who Jesus is? Can we solve the greatest mystery? When Jesus says, "It is finished," we are at the end of the puzzle and the beginning of our quest to understand more fully and deepen our faith. Any new knowledge we gain as a result of our questioning, like Thomas', unveils more of the bright glory of God.

Recommended Resources

Barclay, William. *The Gospel of John*, Vols. 1 and 2 (Daily Study Bible Series). Westminster Press, 1975.

Provides a comprehensive and easy-to-understand commentary on the Gospel of John.

Kysar, Robert. *John's Story of Jesus*. Fortress Press, 1984.

Presents in a simple but lively style the two parts of John's story—Jesus reveals glory and Jesus receives glory. Also discusses the meaning of the major themes of the Gospels and discloses the unity of the whole story.

1

God's Glory Revealed
John 20:30-31
John 2:1-11

This first lesson gives an overview of the theme of mystery and glory in the Gospel of John, shows how John's Gospel differs from the other Gospels, and explores John's way of revealing who Jesus is. In mysterious contrasting images of light and dark, illusion and truth, life and death, John slowly reveals Jesus' identity and what God's purpose is.

Personal Preparation
1. Think about some common signs in your daily life (e.g., road signs, exit signs in a building). How do they point you toward the truth or give you a better understanding of something?
2. Make a list of common contrasts (e.g., day, night; hot, cold; light, dark; up, down). As you study John's Gospel, add other significant contrasts that you find in the text.
3. Reread John 20:30-31 a number of times. Write down in your own words what it means to you. Be brief.
4. Read John 2:1-11. If you had been present at this event, what would your feelings and your response have been to this first sign of Jesus?

Understanding

"In the beginning when God created the heavens and the earth
. . ." (Gen. 1:1). "In the beginning was the Word, and the Word was
with God, and the Word was God" (John 1:1).

The glory and the mystery of God are revealed in the very first
book and the very first verse of the Bible (Gen. 1:1). Then in the
Gospel of John in the New Testament, the glory, wonder, and
mystery of God which were present in the Word now come through
Christ.

While the Synoptic Gospels (Matthew, Mark, and Luke) gradu-
ally reveal who Jesus is, John boldly announces in the very first
sentence of his story that Christ is the incarnation of God. Mark
begins with Jesus' baptism. Matthew and Luke begin with the birth
of Jesus. John begins with the beginning of time and the presence
of the Word with God.

We quickly find out, though, that John's bold claim that Jesus is
the Son of God is very puzzling, mysterious, and sometimes para-
doxical. In the Gospel of John, Jesus promises life through death,
the victory of light over darkness, living water instead of water from
the well, and a Christ who was both fully human and fully divine.
What could Jesus mean by these odd sayings? The solution to these
eternal mysteries, says John, is faith. If we do not believe, the
confusion remains. If we believe through Jesus, we will understand.
Belief is the light that illumines the truth.

The glorious divinity of Christ, which is first seen in the Synoptic
Gospels when Jesus is transfigured, has no beginning for John.
God's presence with us does not begin with Jesus' transfiguration
or even with his birth. For John, it is in the beginning with the Word.
This very spiritual character of John's Gospel and its emphasis on
God's constant revelation distinguishes it from the other three
Gospels.

The mysterious and glorious portrayal of Jesus in the Gospel of
John should not distract us from Jesus' mission to bring us the truth,
however. In John's Gospel, the most important thing is not that water
is turned to wine; the most important thing for John is to reveal who
Jesus really is. Jesus himself is the greatest miracle, breaking into
our time to offer us the truth.

On the face of it, the miracles look like spectacular, supernatural
events. Actually, they are stories that reveal who Jesus is and contrast
God's truth (light, life, heaven, glory) with our illusions of the truth

(darkness, death, earth, humanity). Jesus wants to lead people out of the shadow of illusion into the light of the real world.

Throughout the Gospel we see the strong contrast between truth and illusion in the way Jesus talks. His teachings are often a comparison of our finite, human perceptions with some eternal truth. For instance, he compares our physical need for natural water with our spiritual need for "living water." In another passage, he dispels our agony over death as the end of life and claims that death is actually the joyous beginning of life.

One time, when my husband and I were teaching English in Nanjing, China, under the auspices of the church, we heard a modern-day miracle story that spoke to us of Jesus' truth in contrast to our narrow view of reality. A teacher in a Bible study told us of her husband's experience during the Cultural Revolution. Mr. Wang was jailed because he would not recant his Christianity. The authorities threatened and harassed him night after night in order to keep him awake 24 hours a day, sleep deprivation being one of the most effective methods of brainwashing. Though they tried to make Mr. Wang question reality, he remained strong. Finally, the guard became very angry and shouted, "We'll make you deny your Christ. We'll break you." Mr. Wang replied, "I don't want to deny my Lord. You may force me to deny him with my lips, but you can never force me to deny him in my heart. He is with me and is helping me even now talk with you." After a moment of silence, the guard said quietly, "You are a brave man." Then, a moment later he added, "My grandmother was a Christian." The next day Mr. Wang was released with no explanation.

As in this story, the glory of God is not just something hoped for but a real force that holds us up and sustains us. In this modern story, we see the eternal struggle between light and darkness, truth and falsehood, life and death. But in the end, "the light shines in the darkness, and the darkness did not overcome it" (1:5).

Those who have not known many dark shadows in their lives may have difficulty seeing the contrast between shadow and reality. I am reminded of a young Christian worker from the United States who . naively asked a woman, who had lost her husband and three sons in war, how she could go on believing in God. Maria looked at the young worker and asked, "How could I not believe in God? God is all I have." To the one who lived in an illusion, God was not altogether real. To the one who lived in the light, God was the only thing that was real.

From day to day we all have to choose between illusion and truth. When the war with Iraq began, I turned to the television news to find out what was going on. Feeling that our government had opened Pandora's box by trying to solve a complicated, ancient problem by war, I became depressed. And then, when I had had enough, I found a candle, put it in the center of our table, and vowed anew to focus on my faith and get my news, the good news, from the Lord of life. As with John, God was my reality. I would listen to the television news only once a day and allow myself to be open to how God wanted to use me in these turbulent times. This was my way of choosing to live in the light.

Another contrast in John's Gospel is the juxtaposition of the divine Jesus and the human Jesus. Of all the Gospels, John's portrayal of Jesus is the most divine. Jesus Christ is the perfect revealer of God and speaks with full authority in the Father's name. In 5:19-20, John tells of the relationship between Father and Son in which the Son emanates from the Father. Therefore, people are to honor the Son even as they do the Father.

On the other hand, Jesus is fully human in the Gospel of John. We can relate to him because he is a person like us. In contrast to the glory and majesty of Christ and the deeply spiritual life revealed in John's Gospel, we see a very human Jesus who is weary, thirsty, and hungry—and very much like us. He is disappointed and sorrowful; he weeps. He is joyful and enjoys life. In John's Gospel, Jesus is fully human and fully divine.

This contrast is shown sharply as we move from chapter one, where we have been shown the spiritual Messiah, to the wedding at Cana, an ordinary event, a time of celebration, joy, and laughter. Symbolically important in this story (2:1-11) are the six stone jars. Seven is the perfect number; therefore, six connotes imperfection, perhaps a symbol of imperfect earthly life. These jars, which were to be used for the Jewish rites of purification, each held 20-30 gallons of water. At Jesus' order they were filled to the brim, 120-180 gallons of water in all. Some of it was drawn and taken to the steward. He was bewildered to discover that the content was actually wine, the best wine of the wedding celebration, in fact!

In this story John shows Christ coming into the imperfect world and turning everything upside down. The wine, as we know from our communion services, represents Christ. Here the wine seemingly comes from nowhere and changes everything just as the Divine breaks into our reality and changes everything.

John wants to reveal to us the Christ who not only performed miracles in Palestine many years ago, but is also present and relevant in our lives today. He wants us to see beyond Jesus turning water into wine. He wants us to see that whenever we allow Jesus to come into our lives there is a new quality of life which is *like* turning water into wine. Then life becomes vivid and exciting.

In the summer of 1976, my husband, a schoolteacher, spent six weeks helping with Guatemala's earthquake reconstruction. Just after he came home from Guatemala, he turned right around and left to help shovel mud left by the Johnstown flood. Our 25-year-old niece, who did not at that time go to church, asked wistfully, "Uncle Ivan, how do you get to go and do such exciting things in such interesting times and places?" He replied, "The church gives me these opportunities." "Oh," she said, "I thought church was so dull." She had yet to know the excitement of new life in Christ.

Certainly not everything is thrilling. Shoveling mud is hard work, but the mystery of it all is that, in spite of the mundane, Christ is working in us, changing us, renewing us.

There are times when, even though we have studied and discussed the scriptures for many years, we are like the steward in the wine miracle who cannot see the truth when it is staring him in the face. We need to be more like the servants who knew the source of the wine. They knew who this Jesus was.

One of the ways I try to be more open to Jesus working in my life comes from an American Indian tradition. You may want to try this yourself (or do the exercise in your imagination). First thing in the morning, go outside with a glass of water. Face the west and pray for openness to whatever God has for you that day; take a drink, symbolizing your act of receiving openness. Face the north and pray for wisdom; take a drink symbolizing your act of receiving wisdom. Face the east and pray for new insights and ideas; take a drink symbolizing your act of receiving new insights. Face the south and pray for more trust in God; take a drink symbolizing your act of trusting God. Acknowledge that you have received all these things, and then pour the remaining water on the ground to symbolize your willingness to share what you have received.

John summarizes the lesson of the Gospel in 20:30-31. For those who will accept it, Jesus gives life—not just physical life, but a full life of spirit, truth, and body. Again we see one of John's favorite contrasts: life through Jesus or the alternative, a spiritual death. John tells us that Christ gives an abundant life to those who believe, a peace that passes understanding, a fullness of joy that can only come from Christ. To those who still trust in the rickety powers of this world, as does the steward in 2:9-10, this produces astonishment and bewilderment. To those who believe, Jesus' offer of abundant life produces wonder and awe. We know we are face-to-face with something earthly and ordinary, yet majestic, inspiring, tremendous; something very real and concrete, yet mysteriously indescribable, beyond words.

It is my hope and prayer that, as you study this beloved Gospel, you will each find the excitement and deep satisfaction of uncovering more of the mystery and the glory of God through Jesus Christ, the Son.

Discussion and Action

1. Share some of the many signs common to everyday life. Then discuss the sign of Jesus turning water into wine. To what does this sign point us?
2. In what ways are you like the steward at the wedding, finding it difficult to recognize who Jesus is? How are you like the servants who know who Jesus is? Where do you recognize Jesus today?
3. Name some important contrasts in daily life. Then name some important contrasts in John's Gospel.
4. Recall the stories of Mr. Wang and the author during the war with Iran. Share stories from your life that contrast truth with falsehood, light with darkness.
5. Discuss what it means that Jesus was both fully human and fully divine. Give examples. How difficult is it for you to accept the complete humanity and divinity of Jesus, both fully present at the same time?
6. Ask several people to share their brief statements about John 20:30-31. Suggest that these statements be placed in a prominent place this week (e.g., on the refrigerator door or on a bathroom mirror).
7. Close by singing several verses of "Amazing Grace."

2

Dwelling Among Us
John 1:1-18

In the prologue, the revelation of who Jesus is begins to unfold. Jesus is the Word made flesh, the Word that was with God in the beginning. Jesus lived and worked among the people and still dwells among us today in the form of the Holy Spirit.

Personal Preparation
1. Read John 1:1-18, using different translations/versions of the Bible. Then write paraphrases of several of these passages: verses 1-5, 6-8, 9-13, 14-18. Consider writing one paraphrase in the present tense (e.g., "And the Word becomes flesh and lives with us").
2. Reflect on the meaning of these words from John 1 during the week. What do they say to you in your daily life?
3. What does it mean to dwell with someone? After reflecting on this question, look up the word in a dictionary. Have you ever felt that Jesus Christ dwells with you?

Understanding
John wastes no time getting to the heart of the matter. God was in the beginning, and the Word was with God in the beginning. And then in John 1:1-5 the Word comes alive in a person.

What is a word? And furthermore, what does it mean that the Word lives among us? To us words are very commonplace. Anyone can put their own words into print if they have the money to do so. Many people speak without being conscious of what they are saying. Eliza Doolittle, in *My Fair Lady*, sums up our trivialization of words: "Words, words, words. I'm so sick of words." But a word was very important to the people of Israel. It was far more than a sound; a word had power. It could actually do things.

The Word is at work throughout the Old Testament. In the creation story we read nine times "And God said" and it was done. This repetition emphasizes that God has the power to create simply by uttering a word. God can make anything real.

Then we read in the Book of Isaiah, "Hear the word of the LORD . . . " (1:10; 28:14; 38:4; 39:5; 66:5). In Jeremiah we hear, "Is not my word like fire, says the Lord, and like a hammer that breaks a rock in pieces?" (23:29). The writer of Psalms declares, "By the word of the LORD the heavens were made (33:6).

In Hebrew, the word for "word" is *dabhar,* the creative energy of God. Similarly, in the Greek, the word for "word" is *logos*, the principle that orders and gives meaning to the universe. So John tells us that if we wish to know what the Word is, we should look at Jesus Christ, the creative energy of God.

This creative energy came and lived among us. The Word was made flesh. Just as words make *our* thoughts and *our* wishes concrete, Jesus made the will of God concrete, a real thing that no one had ever seen. God did this for our benefit, bridging the gap between our human nature and the divine Creator.

Julian of Norwich, a mystic of the fourteenth century, thought of Jesus as the link that relates human nature to God. As Jesus, who became human, lives among us, our lives become more godly. We do not become God, but we are joined to God through Jesus Christ.

Matthew Fox, a Dominican scholar, also believes that Jesus unifies us with our Source:

> *There is one flow, one divine energy, one divine word in the sense of one creative energy flowing through all things, all time, all space. We are part of that flow and we need to listen to it.*

God's unity with the people did not fade away when Jesus died. God's creative energy is still available; it dwells with us today in the form of the Holy Spirit. The light still breaks through even when the human darkness of greed, corruption, boredom, or injustice tries to put it out. God's light will not be extinguished. In his book *Original Blessing*, Fox quotes Meister Eckhart who puts it this way: "God is a great underground river that no one can dam up and no one can stop."

In his song for mass, Leonard Bernstein also captures this sense of the ongoing flow of the Word of God. The song comes after the reading of a letter from a young man who is in prison because he refused to go to war. The prisoner says that you can lock people up . . .

> *But you cannot imprison*
> *The Word of the Lord.*
> *No, you cannot imprison*
> *The Word of the Lord.*

Christ, the truly creative Word of God, will not be imprisoned, will not be locked up for long. There is a darkness in our world today—hatred, greed, violence, injustice, and poverty. But this darkness does not have the final say, for God's light breaks through in many individuals and in many situations.

Religion is now accepted in Russia as an integral part of the people's life. Arthur Schnier, president of an interfaith organization working for religious freedom around the world, said, "The Soviet Union, which for 70 years sought to stamp out religion through persecution, repression, and official insistence on atheism, has undergone a complete pro-religious turnabout. Religion is no longer considered the enemy of the state, but its ally."

In a time of great economic and political turmoil, then President Gorbachev called Soviet religious leaders together, seeing "the inherent strength of religious communities as a kind of moral cement to keep the nation together." There has been a tremendous increase in church attendance, which is also true in China, Eastern Europe, and other places. People are searching for a new anchor.

I knew a couple who ran a dairy farm in northern Illinois. They had a global vision and would have loved to travel to the exotic places of which they had heard and read, but they were tied down with their chosen occupation. Since they could not travel to other parts of the world, they brought the world to their home by hosting many international visitors. On one occasion they entertained two Chinese engineers who gladly talked of their country with their hosts. But the visitors had questions, too. One night the four of them stayed up until 2 a.m. talking about faith. The Americans witnessed to their faith and answered the sincere questions their guests had about Jesus and the church.

What an opportunity! Although democracy and freedom are stifled in China now, the church is growing by leaps and bounds. God's light does break through and continues to break through in ways and in places we cannot foresee. As we allow the indwelling Christ to enter our lives, we take on the qualities of his incarnation that include the tasks of healing, celebrating, and co-creating. Our task is to allow the Spirit to work through us.

The Word in the first chapter of John refers to deeds and actions, not just talk. Jesus, the Christ, said "follow me," "receive me," "accept me." These are action words. As the incarnate Christ is within us, then we, too, have the opportunity and responsibility to carry out Christ's work.

Ivan and I spent Christmas Day 1988 with our international friends in Nanjing, China. For two hours in the afternoon, we sang carols we all knew. Then the Dutch sang some of their unique carols, as did the Germans, the Japanese, and the Chinese. One young woman from Uganda, gazing upward and away from the group, sang shyly but clearly "Once in Royal David's City." The Swedish, French, Canadians, British, and some of us from the United States joined in with solos and special favorites. What could have been a time of homesickness became a time in which we experienced the Spirit flowing among us. We left each other full of joy and peace for we were family in a small world.

That special day came to a close leaving each of us with a sense of contentment and satisfaction. But the next day we heard that trouble had broken out at one of the universities on Christmas night, unleashing the tension that had been building between the Chinese and black students. Even though our Ugandan friend, Stella, was not from that university, she was removed from Nanjing temporarily along with about 65 other black students.

Although it was possible that subsequent events might under-mine that feeling of love and goodwill, I wrote to remind Stella that the experience we had on Christmas Day was real. What we had experienced together was a promise of the future when the rule, not the exception, will be to love and care for each other regardless of color, creed, or culture. For, in one small part of the world, God's universal love truly became flesh on Christmas Day, 1988.

Discussion and Action

1. Recall that the words of scripture were originally spoken, not written. Then listen as one person reads aloud John 1:1-18. Invite people to name their favorite part of this well-known text.

2. Share your paraphrases of sections of this text. Ask two or three people to use these paraphrases and put together a group paraphrase of John 1:1-18, to be shared later with the church family—in a newsletter, on a bulletin board, or in worship.

3. How does God's Word *become* flesh today? Be specific: Where do you see God's love and power flowing in your life? in your congregation? in your denomination? in the world?

4. Name some places where God's love and creative energy are being blocked in your life, in your community. What action might your group take to change this, allowing the power of God to move more fully?

5. Listen as one person reads the Christmas Day, 1988, story as told by the author. Then share times when you have also experienced "God's universal love truly becoming flesh."

6. Close by singing "Peace Is Flowing Like a River." At the end, one person speaks: "And all the people said . . . . " All respond: "Amen! Amen! Amen!"

3

The World: To Love or Reject?
John 3:16-17; 17:13-23

Loving the world so much, God sent a Son to live on earth. The Son of God calls us to live in the world but, in a different way, in the kingdom. The kingdom is not a place of perfection, but where the truth about God and Jesus are known.

Personal Preparation

1. What are some parts of the world (the earth and its people) that you truly love?
2. Is there some part of the world that you hate, very much dislike, or with which you feel uncomfortable?
3. Read the two scripture passages above. In light of them, do you feel Christians have any responsibility to do something about their hates, dislikes, or uncomfortable feelings about the world?

Understanding

Jesus proclaims God's love for the world over and over again. It is like a parent's love for a child. If we accept John 3:16, then we accept that God loves us, each one. As we who are human love our children, so much more does God, our heavenly Father, love us. Each of us holds a secure place in God's heart. It matters to God what we become and what becomes of us. The glory of this love was beautifully stated by the twelfth-century mystic Hildegard of Bingen

when she wrote, "God hugs you. You are encircled by the arms of
the mystery of God." Loving us so much, God sent Jesus to deliver
God's message of grace and to save the world from self-destruction.
And for the same reason, Jesus commissioned the disciples, who
seemed ill-prepared to do much of anything, to go into the world to
offer God's grace and salvation.

Christ accepted the disciples as intimate friends and co-workers.
Moreover, he considered anyone who believed in him and did the
will of God in the world to be disciples also. As we modern-day
believers accept the love of God, we are all members of one family
(17:21). Christ's prayer is that in oneness we will know our relationship not only to Christ but to each other. All believers in Christ will
be united in purpose and in love like a family.

Jesus also commissions us, as he did the beloved disciples, to be
sent into the world to proclaim the good news. But when Jesus says
that the disciples are not of the world as he is not of the world (John
17:14), we are a bit confused. Were they too worldly or other-
worldly? In actuality, the disciples seem very worldly. The world
that entices and ensnares has no appeal for Jesus, but the disciples
often gave in to temptation.

Most accounts of the disciples show them to be far from perfect.
In the Gospel of Matthew they cling to their material dreams of an
earthly kingdom and their prominence in it. They are ambitious,
vying for position (Matt. 20:21). But in John's Gospel, the disciples
do not believe that the kingdom is a place or that their own personal
piety or favor with Jesus can earn them a position in it. In John's
Gospel, what is most important is what people believe and how
much they understand. The kingdom is a full disclosure of the truth,
the solution to the eternal mysteries of God, and a knowledge of
who God is. The greater the disciples' knowledge, the closer to God
they are.

Jesus knows that, in spite of their weaknesses, these men are
different from people of the world, and he gives them credit for it.
There are, of course, many other men and women who believe Jesus.
They are able to live in this imperfect world, yet belong to another
reality, the world of truth and knowledge about God.

After Jesus was gone in human form and embodied by the
church, first-century Christians tried to live in the world but not of
it as Jesus prescribed (John 17:14-16). They would not serve in
armies, wear uniforms, or hold slaves. They would not conform to

the logic of the world though they were in it. Instead, they subscribed to God's truth and tried to live by it.

Many groups of Christians since the early church have tried to live according to Jesus' model. One example is the Church of the Brethren, which has taught nonconformity to the world's standards from their very beginning in 1708 in Schwarzenau, Germany. After the bloody Thirty Years War in Europe and rampant corruption in the state church, the people were weary of the world's way of doing things; so the early Brethren tried to live up to the calling to live in the world but not of it.

Nonconformity has been a very controversial issue for Christians over the years. For some, Jesus' way is an ideal to strive for but one which can never be fully achieved. For them nonconformity is unrealistic. Others believe that only a life patterned closely after Christ's is a Christian life, and for them nonconformity is essential. Still others look toward life in the hereafter, and for them the matters of this world are futile; neither conformity nor nonconformity matters to them.

Voluntary service agencies sponsored by churches sometimes ask recruits to take up a life of nonconformity. Volunteers sacrifice their comfort, their incomes, their security in the world to live the life of the kingdom. If asked why they agree to live at a poverty level, many volunteers answer, "It is our faith." By serving others, the way is open to share their faith. In a time when self-improvement, careers, and success are the way of the world, these people are true nonconformists. But they do not reject the world entirely. They serve the world without adopting its standards of success, happiness, violence, and power.

It is difficult to be in the world but not of it. Our comparatively wealthy lifestyles in the United States subtlety draw us into the world's standards. We may actually be unaware of how deeply our ways are immersed in the world. One day we become aware and see we can no longer conform to the world. But this also wakens us to the realization that to separate from the world's ways will be costly; and we're not sure we want to give up our comforts, our good friends, and possibly our jobs.

One of the subtle ways we conform to the world is through the payment of taxes. Most Christians accept our civic responsibility and pay as the law requires. We would be in big trouble if we didn't. But I know some very capable families who choose not to earn more money than they need to survive so they will not be required to pay income tax. They especially oppose the use of their tax money (as much as 54 percent) for military spending; very little goes to the poor whom our Lord taught us to help. These families choose to be in the world but are, decidedly, not of it.

Not only adults but also children choose Jesus' way over the ways of the world. In February 1991, during the war in the Persian Gulf, with its frenzy of flag-waving patriotism, our six-year-old grand-daughter came home from school to say she needed to wear a red, white, and blue T-shirt the next day to show support for the troops. Her mother said she could if she wanted to, but first she explained to her how she herself felt about the war. She explained how she cared about the troops and their families. She also cared about the Iraqis who were being killed (the figure may now be as high as 200,000). She did not support what the troops were being ordered to do. The next morning Carrie came downstairs wearing a red, white, and blue T-shirt and black pants. She said, "The T-shirt is to show I care about the soldiers and their families. The black pants show I don't like what our government is doing."

When we finally accept God's call to be in but not of the world, we still struggle. We are so much a part of the world we find it difficult to really see God's way. The life of nonconformity draws criticism and ridicule, testing our endurance. We retreat a little, knowing that even the disciples failed, at times, to embrace Jesus' way. We are quick to point out that Thomas doubted Jesus' logic and Peter bumbled the meaning of Jesus' teachings.

Imperfect though we are, we are encouraged to pursue Jesus' way when we hear the stories of other Christians struggling with non-conformity. During the civil war in Nicaragua, thousands of Christians from all over the world went into that tiny country to help the people. A Swiss agronomist working there told his wife that he loved the Nicaraguan children so much he would gladly give his life if he could save one of those little ones. He and his wife were just completing a long-term assignment and were looking forward to returning to Switzerland and starting a family of their own. But one day there was a knock at the door. It was some of the women and children who had been on a march with the Swiss couple that day. Their truck had broken down and they asked if they could rest before walking home. Maurice said he would take them in his truck since it was not safe for them to walk. On the way, the truck hit a land mine. As they ran from the truck, the contras fired upon them. Later Maurice's bullet-riddled body was found sheltering and protecting two children who were still alive. He saved not one but two Nicaraguan children.

Father Miguel D'Escoto, a Nicaraguan Maryknoll priest, born and educated in the United States, was Nicaragua's foreign minister from 1979 to 1990. He says this about living in the world but not of it:

> *If I refused to help my wounded people for fear that Maryknoll might expel me, how would I explain that to my Lord? . . . The cross is the inevitable consequence of preaching the fatherhood of God and a communion of sisters and brothers among all human beings, and denouncing everything that keeps this communion from becoming a reality. . . . the cross is life. . . . life can't be measured in the number of days an existence lasts, but by the depth of a commitment. (*Teofilo Cabestero, Ministers of God, Ministers of the People*)

Father D'Escoto's question is our question also. How can we, as believers, resist the evils of the world that surround us and also love the world and work in it?

Discussion and Action

1. Share honestly some of the parts of the world you "truly love" and other parts you "very much dislike."
2. How can Christians live out the paradox in Christ's command that we be "in the world" but not "of the world"?
3. Do you think that Christians today are too worldly, too materialistic, too comfortable in their lifestyles? Give reasons for your answers.
4. Name some actions your covenant group could take in the next three months that would reflect your being "in the world but not of it." Decide on one such action that you will do as a group.
5. Listen as one person reads aloud Jesus' words as given in John 17:20-23. Then name some of the divisions and differences between believers. What are some differences in thought and belief within your own group? How is the

unity of Christ still possible among believers? in your own group?

6. Learn from a role play. Have volunteers dramatize the following scene:

After careful consideration, a young couple with three children, ages one to five, purchase a home on the edge of the inner city in a mixed neighborhood. One reason for their move is to witness to the grace of God. This place becomes home to them, and they like the neighborhood. Some people in their church, however, feel it is too dangerous for them, that it would be better if they move. One day their house is broken into and some valuable things are taken. Three weeks later another attempt is made. Police believe the break-ins are drug-related and involve people from a neighboring block.

Dramatize this couple talking with several friends from church about what they should do. Following the role play, discuss it as a group.

7. Close with moments of silence. Then sing as a prayer: "Into my heart, into my heart, come into my heart, Lord Jesus. Come in today; come in to stay; come into my heart, Lord Jesus."

4

"I AM . . ."
John 8:12
John 15:1-8

John further reveals Jesus' true identity using the famous "I am" statements. Only those who truly know Jesus understand the seemingly odd comparisons of Jesus to a door, to bread, to a vine, and to water.

Personal Preparation
1. Look up seven distinct "I am" statements of Jesus, found in John's Gospel: John 6:35, 48; 8:12; 10:7-9, 11, 14; 11:25; 14:6; 15:1, 5.
2. What pattern do you see in these statements? Do you see one main idea throughout these verses?
3. Write some simple symbolic statements that help you understand who Jesus is (e.g., Jesus is the road map; Jesus is a refreshing rain after a long drought).
4. Read aloud John 15:1-8 at different times this week. Think about "abiding in Jesus' love" as you go about your work.

Understanding
In the story of Moses and the burning bush (Exod. 3), Moses asks what he should call God. God says, "I AM WHO I AM. . . . Thus you shall say to the Israelites, 'I AM has sent me to you' " (v. 14).

Echoing God's proclamation in Exodus, Jesus says, "I am the light," "I am the door," "I am the bread," "I am the shepherd," "I am the living water." The similarity between Jesus, who calls himself "I am," and God, who declares "I AM WHO I AM," signifies that Jesus has a divine origin in God and a divine mission to the world. Regardless of the clarity and forthrightness of Jesus' claims, however, the people do not understand him or who he is. They are constantly bewildered or in conflict with Jesus, and eventually they destroy the man they cannot understand.

In the Gospel of John, only those who believe in Jesus can understand who he is. Most encounters in the gospel leave people confused. They do not know that Jesus is from God or that he offers them the essentials of all life. They think they have everything they need. The only things required in life, they think, are common things such as bread, water, light, and shelter. It is true that these basic elements are necessary to life, but unless we also have these things in Christ, we are dead spiritually. Our physical survival depends on the spiritual necessities as well. We must have both for a joy-filled, abundant life in Christ.

For a culture such as ours that searches constantly for meaning in things, jobs, and other people, yet still feels hungry for a purpose in life, Jesus is the essential ingredient we are missing.

Jesus teaches how to live joyfully and abundantly, and so to reject Jesus is to reject the essentials of life. To accept Jesus is to accept life. Those who recognized who Jesus was knew what he meant when he said "I am the bread" or "I am the vine."

In John 15:1-8, Jesus speaks to his followers who already believe and know who Christ is. He paints a vivid picture of his relationship to the Father and to his followers. He gives us an image of the mystical union between Christ and Christians, using the imagery of the vine and the branches. Christ is the vine and believers are the branches joined to him.

The union with Christ does not depend on one's citizenship, race, family, creed, or class. The only thing that matters is whether a person believes in Jesus or "knows" Jesus. Like the branch, the believers who stay near their source will thrive.

To know God is to love God as Jesus did, and to love God is to be on fire, to reach out to whomever we're called so that others can know of God's love. For it is impossible to keep this love to oneself. Jesus says that the proof of discipleship is to bear much fruit (John

15:8). This does not necessarily mean counting the numbers of those who have been added to the church rolls. To share the faith is a way of life and God will take it from there. The key to bearing fruit is to remain united to Jesus, the source of all life.

This friendship then, this union with Christ, is realized in loving service. When we go on our own strength, we miss the boat.

When we stray too far from the branch, we are like the woman who tried to build a church by herself. She was a member of a church that was built in a new housing development. It seemed to this woman that the evangelism committee was slow to invite new members. She felt members should be visiting door-to-door in the neighborhood. Angry and upset with the others, she set out on her own with a zeal that conveyed the attitude "I'll show them." When the minister went calling, time and again he heard of the angry woman who had come ahead of him, already turning some people off to the church.

In contrast, the church in China, which stays close to the branch, is growing by leaps and bounds. I heard newcomers to the church in China say over and over of the Christians, "They are so kind." The churches are full every Sunday morning. Children must sit on adults' laps. Chairs are put in the aisles and along the sides of the room. One Sunday morning I saw 120 people being baptized. These are the fruits of those who abide near the branches, those who exemplify a life with Jesus at the center.

Jesus uses the imagery of the vine and branches when speaking to his followers who believe and understand who Christ is. To nonbelievers, however, Jesus says who he is in a simple way, comparing himself to ordinary objects and hoping the people will understand. He says, for instance, "I am the light." Light exposes things. In the light we can see the world for what it really is.

Jesus also said, "I am the bread of life." Much of our lives revolve around food. We work to pay for it, we want it fast, we want it to have few calories, no cholesterol. We want it in great variety. We spend time growing it, shopping for it, fixing it. We have special food for special occasions. Great decisions are made at the dinner table over food, and food is the center of courtships and companionship, industry and trade. But food alone does not sustain us. Jesus is the prime sustaining force in our lives. Without him and our relationship to God, our food is of no value.

In the movie "The Long Walk Home," which dramatizes the Montgomery bus boycotts of the 1950s, a group of maids walk to work instead of taking segregated buses. Despite the long walk home after work to face a mountain of work in their own households, the women go to worship at night. Close to exhaustion, they drag themselves to church. There they sing, and as they sing their fatigue is replaced by strength and courage. As they take in the rich life-giving source, they are filled and renewed for the struggle. The bread of life nourishes them in a way that food cannot.

Jesus, the light of the world, shines a light on the truth. Jesus, the bread of life, feeds our spirits. Jesus also provides an opening, a way to God. He says, "I am the door." When we come up against walls in our lives and it seems impossible to break through, we have to wait for Jesus to open the door. No matter how impossible a situation, there is a way through it.

When Jesus talks with the woman at the well (John 4), he offers yet another seemingly ordinary thing, water. At first, she is one of the people who is confused by Jesus' mysterious way of speaking. She understands his offer literally, but not as he intended it. Jesus repeats the offer in an even more vivid way. "Everyone who drinks of this water will be thirsty again, but those who drink of the water that I will give them will never be thirsty" (4:13-14). Still she fails to comprehend that Jesus is the "living water," the source of life. Finally Jesus compels the woman to discover and face the truth for herself. When she realizes she is speaking to Christ, she goes back to the city and says to the people, "Come and see . . . " (4:28-29).

Knowing Jesus is not something we can be taught. It is not something we can know from reading or study. It is something we must discover for ourselves. A reporter was interviewing the well-known psychiatrist Dr. Carl G. Jung, who was in his late seventies. The reporter asked, "Dr. Jung, do you believe in God?" Dr. Jung thought a while and then answered slowly, "Do I believe in God? No. I don't believe. I know."

The people Jesus encounters lack spiritual vision. But God's divine initiative is at work. It is by the grace of God that people are able to have faith. It is truly the Lord's will that all who see God's glory as revealed in Christ will possess the real life that Christ offers. This glory promises joy, not frothy and frilly joy but a deeply satisfying joy, and a life with enabling power.

The key to life for Jesus was his contact with God. Time and again he withdrew to nurture this relationship. Russians have a word *Poustinia* ("Pou-" rhymes with "you"), which means "desert." But it is more than a geographical place; it means a quiet, lonely place that people may enter to find the God who dwells within them. Catherine de Hueck Doherty, in her book *Poustinia*, writes:

> *If we are to witness to Christ in today's marketplaces, where there are constant demands on our whole person, we need silence. . . . The silence is the search of man [and woman] for God. . . . True silence is a suspension bridge that a soul in love with God builds to cross the dark, frightening gullies of its own mind . . . the depthless precipices of its own fears that impede its way to God. . . . True silence is a key to the immense and flaming heart of God.*

Mrs. Doherty goes on to say that the world indeed knows about God. But because it only knows *about* God and doesn't understand who God is, the world can reject God through ignorance or by indifference. The world can recrucify God a thousand times a day in a neighbor. "But if the world knew God through his own revelation of himself to us in the *poustinia* of our hearts, then it could not reject God. . . . Then love would enter the world through us."

The Great I AM came to us in the form of one of our own who spoke our language. Through everyday images of water, bread, light, vines, and doors, we are able to know who this God is. Better yet, if we eat of the bread, drink of the water, live in the light, enter through the door, and abide near the vine, we can do more than know God. We can share whole and abundant life with him.

Discussion and Action

1. Share your statements about Jesus that help you understand who he is and what he means for your life.
2. Recall the seven "I am" statements Jesus made. Ask each person to name a favorite one or two of these and tell why it is so important.
3. Describe an occasion when you went, tired and reluctantly, to a meeting and found yourself energized and uplifted. Discuss what happened: Did this result from something

you did, something someone else did, or was it part of the mystery of the Spirit?

4. Ask people to name a need or a want they now have. Then look at this need or want through the eyes of Christ. What are some possible next steps?

5. Share in a meditation time. Listen as one person quietly reads John 15:1-8. Then picture in your mind the grapevine and branches as Jesus and you. Or you may choose a beautiful setting with Jesus walking with you. Talk with Jesus about your life right now, your joys, your pains, your needs. Listen to Jesus' words to you. Relax and let yourself be/abide in Jesus.

6. Have one person close the meditation and this session by reading Jesus' words, "I have said these things . . . so that my joy may be in you, and that your joy may be complete" (John 15:11).

5

Jesus Christ: The Way
John 14:1-13

Jesus is the way to faith; and the way is a path of understanding. We are to have a questioning spirit like that of Thomas whose role was to learn, to find out, and to probe. Only as students and imitators of Christ will we learn the way.

Personal Preparation
1. Recall a time when as a child you were lost or afraid you were lost. What were your feelings? What happened?
2. Think about how the people of Israel, throughout their history, spoke of "the way." "This is the way; walk in it" (Isa. 30:21). Read Psalm 1 and reflect on these words about "the way."
3. Read John 14:1-13. Ask yourself: What is Jesus' way? What does it mean for me to walk in his way?

Understanding
In these opening verses of John 14, Jesus talks about the future and where he is going. He tells the disciples, "You know the way to the place where I am going" (14:4). But Thomas confronts Jesus, saying they don't know the way; how could they possibly know the way? Thomas is often called the doubter because he never accepts anything, not even Jesus' teachings, without making sure he under-

stands. So he asks questions, not to be cantankerous, but to better understand. He might even be called Thomas, the searcher.

Whatever we call him, Thomas helps us to ask questions freely. When he doesn't understand what Jesus is saying about the way, he decides it is better to ask questions than to dismiss Jesus as a fool. Thomas says, "Lord, we do not know where you are going. How can we know the way?" (14:5). Jesus responds again with an "I am" statement saying, "I am the way." Jesus, himself, is the way to God. He is the truth of God. Thomas's searching questions help us uncover the mystery of Jesus. So for John who says that the way to faith is through understanding, Thomas is an important character.

Like Thomas, we grope for an answer to the question, How can a person be "the way"? I am reminded of the time my husband and I were driving through St. Johns, New Brunswick, and could not find our destination. We were lost. Ivan pulled the car into a side street and stopped. Soon another car pulled in behind us. The woman walked up to our car and asked if she could help us, so we told her where we wanted to go. She gave us directions, but because of a number of one-way streets, there would be many twists and turns in the route. Finally she said, "It will be better if I lead the way and you follow." She not only told us the way but, in a very real sense, she became the way. So it is with Jesus. He not only has taught us about and lived the way, he actually is the way itself. He walks with us, strengthening and enabling us to fully live each day.

Gazing out my window, I also think of how first-time visitors could lose their way in the thick woods surrounding our house. There is a path, a way through the brush and trees; however, one could wander from the path and get scratched, cut, hurt, lost. But the path is still there. One only needs to find the path again to be on one's way. For us, Jesus is the constant, consistent way. The more we walk in this way, the better we understand our special relationship to God, Christ, and the Spirit. The more clearly we see the way we are to walk, the more meaningful is our personal relationship to Christ, so much so that we can ask anything in his name.

This seems so simple, yet it is very difficult. What does "Jesus, the way," mean in our everyday practical lives? What is the way of Jesus? We know that God's way is love. "God so loved the world that he gave his only Son . . . " (3:16). Christ is one with the Father, which means that he, too, follows the way of love. And we are to know our oneness with the Father through Jesus, so we are to love. The way of Christ is the way of love.

At first, it may seem easy to accept this, for we love our families, friends, and others, especially those who think the same way we do. The difficulty begins with those who think differently than we do even in the church, to say nothing about those outside the church who look and act quite differently. Jesus' way is to love. "Just as I have loved you, you also should love one another" (John 13:34). Jesus demonstrates the breadth of this command when he dares to offer living water to a Samaritan woman, whom Jews considered an enemy. He follows the most difficult way of love when he heals the ear of the soldier who came to arrest him. He loves his own people who hate and reject him.

Jesus' way is to reach out in love and compassion to all kinds of people, including Gentiles and the hated Samaritans. Yet, at the same time we hear Jesus say: "I am the way, and the truth, and the life. No one comes to the Father except through me" (John 14:6). Does this mean that Jesus' way is the only one? What does this say about other faiths or religions?

We have struggled for a long time with the conflicting examples of Jesus' offer of grace for the faithful only and his love for the non-believer. This, too, is part of the mystery of Jesus that we must grapple with, being open to fuller understanding of God's truth.

It is clear that Jesus served all people with humble dignity. To walk in Christ's way is to walk humbly—not arrogantly, to be willing to do the dirty work in this world, and to serve the unlovely people of God. We cannot walk in Christ's way when our attitudes proclaim that we think we are better or more faithful than others. Indeed, some non-Christians may be following the way more closely than Christians who are paternalistic or racist or arrogant.

In contrast to this tarnished image of Christians, I. W. and Mabel Moomaw, agricultural missionaries for the Church of the Brethren in India, presented a truly Christian image of humble service. They shared their expertise in the non-Christian world, taking care at all times to respect the beliefs and values of the people among whom they lived. I. W. was so highly respected in India that the nation honored him by awarding him the Emperor's Gold Award for Distinguished Service in India.

Jesus' words cause even committed Christians to reflect on and search our hearts for the way in which we are walking. Jesus invited anyone, not just the repentant ones but also the believers, to walk the way. "Let anyone who is thirsty come to me." In Matthew 25, Jesus paints a picture of those who do God's will and those who do not. He says that whenever we feed the hungry, give a drink to the thirsty, welcome the stranger, clothe the naked, visit the sick and those in prison, we are doing it to Christ.

To know Jesus' way and to walk in it is a growing experience. There is so much to learn and understand that we cannot grasp it all. It takes a lifetime of learning. Yet, too often, we act as though we know it all. This attitude leads to judgmental attitudes toward those who are different or think differently than we do. When we think "My way is the only right way," we are linking Christ's way to our own thinking and our own way.

In her book *Walking on Water*, Madeline L'Engle writes:

> *We human beings too often tend to codify God, to feel we know where he is and where he is not, and this arrogance leads to such things as the Spanish inquisition, the Salem witch burnings and has the result of further fragmenting an already broken Christendom.*

We have observed and, no doubt, have discovered for ourselves that to walk in Jesus' way is not easy. How do we do it? If we open our hearts to the world God has created and begin to understand his purpose, we will find thankfulness and love flowing from us in much the same way that Etty Hillesum describes in her diary, *An Interrupted Life*. Etty Hillesum, a young woman who was killed at the age of 29 in the concentration camp at Auschwitz, writes:

> *The misery here is quite terrible and yet, late at night when the day has slunk away into the depths behind me, I often walk with a spring in my step along the barbed wire and then time and again it soars straight from my heart—I can't help it, that's just the way it is, like some elementary force—the feeling that life is glorious and magnificent, and that one day we shall be building a whole new world. Against every new outrage and every fresh horror we shall put up one more piece of love and goodness.*

Jesus talked over and over again of joy. Just before his death, he prayed that the disciples "may have my joy fulfilled in themselves." Jesus' way is not a grim, sour-faced, guilt-ridden way. It's a joyous way.

The path is before us, but this pathway to abundant living isn't always easy. However, when we're open to seeing and hearing, we will find the way and we will be able to walk it joyfully.

Isaiah said, "This is the way, walk in it." Jesus said, "I am the way."

Discussion and Action

1. Share memories of being physically lost or thinking you were lost.

2. Recall a time in the past two years when you were lost—in confusion, anxiety, or despair. How did you find your way to peace and clarity? Share some of these experiences.

3. Name people you know who "walk in the way of Jesus." What qualities do they have that identify them as "followers of the way"?

4. What individuals or groups do you think may be excluded from Jesus' way? Who decides who is "in" and who is "out"?

5. Do you have difficulty including certain people or groups as part of "the way"? How do you feel that Jesus wants you to relate to them?

6. What does "walking in Jesus' way" mean for you right now? Write down two or three specific ideas and share them with your group, if you like. Consider also whether there is one thing that your whole group might do that reflects "walking in his way."

7. Close with prayers that you may walk in Jesus' way this week. Then sing together: "I've got peace like a river . . . joy like a fountain . . . love like an ocean, in my soul."

6

Jesus Christ: The Truth
John 14:6; 8:31-47

*In the Gospel of John, the truth of faith does not appear
suddenly; it unfolds. Disciples of Jesus make their way
little by little to the kernel of truth that is hidden under
layers and layers of meaning. Faith deepens as we quest
for it and open ourselves to learning new truth.*

Personal Preparation
1. Remember your specific commitment to "walk in Jesus'
   way" this week. How are you doing?
2. Read the above scriptures, and then read John 18:33-38.
3. Pilate asks Jesus, "What is truth?" Reflect on this important question. What is truth to you? Is real truth ever
   dangerous or misleading? Is it freeing? In what way is Jesus
   the truth in your life?

Understanding
Throughout history great teachers have taught lasting truths, but
no teacher except Jesus could embody the truth. Only Jesus could
say "I am the truth." Moral truth must be conveyed by words and it
must be shown by example. This is where even the greatest human
teacher falls down. No teacher has ever completely lived according
to his or her own teachings except Jesus. Many can say, "I have
taught you the truth." Jesus can say, "I am the truth."

In chapter 8, John reports Jesus' promise: "If you continue in my word . . . you will know the truth and the truth will set you free" (John 8:31-32). What does it mean to "continue in [his] word"? For John the truth does not come in a flash; it must be uncovered layer by layer. We have to feel around for the pearl in the oyster; it doesn't just sit on top in plain sight. If we continue in Jesus' way, we will uncover more and more of the truth, never understanding it completely.

Too many Christians have crossed the border into Christ's kingdom and traveled no farther. We haven't continued in the word. There is no pressing on for us, no striving for the fullness that is there for all. Many never grow up in Christ. Too many of us are content to stay safe just inside the door without venturing farther. Little do we know, there is no level of knowledge at which we are "in." The moment we think we know the truth is the moment we realize there is a lot to learn. As we open ourselves to the mystery of Christ, experiencing him personally, we grow deeper and deeper in our faith. Those who are open to learning more are like the college freshman who felt he knew everything and his father was so dumb; by the time he graduated, he was amazed how smart his father had become in four years!

As we continue to grow in the word, we realize how the truth sets us free. When one of our daughters was about five years old, she had a playmate who told lies. The little girl seemingly knew nothing else. We very quickly found out that our daughter was learning to lie from her friend so we curtailed her privileges. She could not go half a block away to another friend's house because we could not trust her. This phase did not last long, however, because lying was not ingrained in her, and she learned quickly that truth breeds trust and results in freedom.

On the other hand, there was an auto collision repair man who gave estimates to insurance companies based on the cost of new parts. Then he would actually straighten out and fix the old parts, painting them to look like new. Although this man succeeded in selling used parts for new ones for several years, he was eventually sued by the defrauded customers and their insurance companies. There was an obvious lack of trust from the public and business declined. He certainly found no freedom in dishonesty.

At the same time, another auto collision repair man was operating the busiest and most successful repair business in the city. He was a committed Christian businessman who provided dependable work, good prices, and honest dealings. The truth set him free to be and do the best work he could do and to make his business dealings a continuing witness to his strong faith. Sin enslaves us, but the truth sets us free.

Christ truly can and does work with us in breaking the bonds of sin, but we have to recognize our own slavishness to sin in order to be freed from it. More often than not, we are like the Jews of John's Gospel who do not understand the truth. We recognize ourselves in their failure to believe Jesus, in their defensiveness for tradition, and in their frequent confusion. However, the more we work with Jesus, the more we, like they, know the truth. The more we know, the freer we become.

As Christians we sometimes refuse to hear the truth. When I was a child I was given a blotter stamp with three monkeys pictured on it. Under the monkeys it said, "Hear no evil, see no evil, speak no evil." This may be all right for children, but it is not healthy for adults to close their eyes and mouths to what is going on.

For too long people in the United States have wanted to believe that everything is all right in our country. We know there are big problems, but they have affected "those people over there." We have not been hurt too much. We have wanted to believe our leaders when they have told us our economy is just fine, but, of course, we know some people have been laid off. We don't want to hear that, after years of being the biggest lender nation in the world, we have become the largest debtor nation in the world.

By living a lie, we are held in bondage to falsehoods. Furthermore, our collaboration allows the perpetrator to keep on lying. For instance, as long as we believe the economy is healthy, we will not be overly alarmed when our government keeps borrowing, even though in 1990 six percent of our national income was used to pay the interest on the burgeoning debt.

When we, the citizens, face the truth, we can begin to help each other and our government leaders deal with the problems. "If you continue in my word . . . you will know the truth, and the truth will make you free."

As Christians who are trying to live in the world, but not of it, we need to realize anew that many of us have too often allowed ourselves to accept as truth what we see on television and read in the newspapers. Often we do not bother to question suspicious claims or listen to our brothers' and sisters' experiences in other lands, such as El Salvador, Nicaragua, Israel, and Iraq. Too many Christians naively believe that our presidents and our government leaders would not lie.

The sad reality is that it is often difficult to find the truth. Oliver North epitomizes our times when, in the Iran-Contra hearings, he admitted that "he lied repeatedly to Congress, acknowledged that he knew lying was wrong, but insisted that it never occurred to him that he was violating the law" (*Opening Arguments*, Jeffrey Toobin). The lying all around us can be very subtle. Even as it was hard for people in biblical times to hear Jesus, it is just as hard for us to hear him today.

We have a Christ who can empower us to face anything. We can even face the hard truth about ourselves. We can deal with the truth because Jesus, himself, is the truth, and loving him we can love the truth. If the truth hurts, the freedom it affords heals us and frees us to look openly at ourselves, our country, and our world. It does not mean we have to abandon the world. Just as Jesus was in the Roman world but not of it, so we are in our own world but, hopefully, not of it. Jesus says, "Whoever is from God hears the word of God" (8:47a). We, who are of God, listen!

Dishonesty and lying may win out temporarily, but they cannot sustain themselves forever. In China, after the massacre in Tienanmen Square, the open news reporting stopped immediately and only official government news was allowed. Over and over the people heard the government version of the incident reporting that students had killed a large number of soldiers while government troops had killed only a few students (20-30). The people didn't believe the government news. The Communist Party, already distrusted, bankrupted itself morally that day, June 4, 1989. Right now the Communist Party has the upper hand, but underneath there is a movement. Truth and freedom will someday break forth. A newspaper article in the Fort Wayne (Indiana) *Journal-Gazette*, March 16, 1991, states:

> *Growing numbers of Communist Party members have turned to religion and are going to church or the temple instead of party meetings, the Peasants' Daily, an official newspaper, reported this week. Religious activities compete with party activities for people . . . damaging*

> *the party's image . . . seriously influencing party build-*
> *ing at the basic village level. In one county, in central*
> *Hebei province, only 270 people joined the party last*
> *year, while 813 became Christian.*

In our own country we've had to face up to the My Lai village massacre in Vietnam and its massive cover-up. We've had to deal with the fact that the bombings in Panama killed over 1,000 innocent women and children. Where is the truth? Truth is not just what we want it to be or what some charismatic leader tells us it is. Truth is Jesus Christ—his standards, his values, his teachings.

During World War I, the United States claimed that Germans went into Belgium and cut off little children's hands. Nothing like that really happened, but the story was used to whip up war hysteria. It has been noted that "truth is the first casualty of war." War distorts, twists, and crucifies the truth.

Christ's truth does not destroy. It liberates. Christ's truth does not threaten. We, the followers of Christ, have an opportunity to stand for truth. Often it won't be popular. Truth can make us lonely; the truth can make us cry. But Jesus never said truth would be easy and popular. He never said it would make us happy. He said it will make us free. God is still at work bringing hope out of the worst things people do. Joyce Hollyday, writing in *Sojourners*, shares:

> *Missionary friends just back from five years in Laos*
> *have brought home pictures of seedlings growing in the*
> *casings of bombs that were dropped in the last US war*
> *that ravaged Southeast Asia. Other pictures show bomb*
> *casings transformed into prosthetic limbs for children,*
> *to replace legs blown off by land mines. Such poignancy*
> *speaks to the indomitable nature of the human spirit.*
> *And the presence of God in history. Lest we forget.*

What is truth? Jesus Christ is the truth. His values, his way, his teachings are all a part of the truth. Truth is the ultimate reality—the divine reality embodied in Jesus Christ.

Discussion and Action

1. Share with the group how you have kept your specific commitments to "walk in Jesus' way."

2. Share your own personal definitions of truth and how you see Jesus being the truth for you.

3. What do you think the author means by "the truth can make us lonely . . . make us cry"? What truths about yourself, your church community, the world, make you feel lonely or sad or bring tears?

4. What pockets of pride in your life blind you to God's truth? What pride as a nation might blind us to God's truth?

5. Discuss how we can more fully discover God's truth in the news reports about our world. What sources do you use to find such truth? Bring to the group some magazines or periodicals that provide a different perspective on the "truth" about news events or ways of understanding life (e.g., *Christian Science Monitor, Sojourners, Washington Spectator, Fellowship* [from Fellowship of Reconciliation], and denominational magazines).

6. When have you known the freedom that comes from facing the truth about yourself or about the world? Share some of these "freeing truth" times.

7. Close with a quiet time: Sing "Kum Ba Yah." Then sing: "Come by here, my Lord, come by here. . . . " Then sing: "Help us know the truth, kum ba yah. . . . O Lord, come by here." Give time for silent prayers, and close with the leader saying, "And all the people said . . . " and all responding, "Amen! Amen! Amen!"

7

Jesus Christ: The Life
John 10:7-10; 14:6; 17:1-5

Not only does Jesus show the way to a life full of purpose, he is life to all who follow him. He brings eternal life, abundant life, life to the full, a life of knowledge and truth. Eternal life is not just a style of life, it is a quality of life.

Personal Preparation
1. Look for pictures that speak to you of fullness of life; take them to the group meeting.
2. Read the scriptures. Then ponder this: What does it mean to live an abundant life—life to the full, life overflowing?
3. Eternal life is described in John 17:3, as "[knowing] the only true God and Jesus Christ." Is this possible now as well as after death?
4. When have you personally experienced Jesus Christ as the life?

Understanding
Most people are looking for meaning in life, for satisfaction, for purpose. It is possible, of course, to drift along, satisfying one's hungers and wants, hoping for the best, yet not believing in much. It is not possible, however, to be wholly at peace or wholly alive without a vital faith in something beyond oneself. We are made for

something more. It is part of being human. The principal way we enlarge our lives is by accepting Jesus who says, "I am . . . the life."

The search for happiness, which people often restlessly pursue, is not just for new experiences or pleasure; it's for something that will make life worth living. After a young man fell in love, he said, "I never knew what life was until I saw it through your eyes." Living for others brings us life. That is what Jesus does. Jesus shows us that a life for God is a life worth living. It is life indeed.

The abundant life, of which Christ speaks, is not measured by material possessions. He is talking about a plentiful supply of love, gentleness, forgiveness, joy, peace, grace, truth, and power. A full life of meaning involves knowing God and reaching out, sharing that knowledge with others. Christ is not a miserly, stingy, or begrudging giver. He gives abundantly, full to overflowing.

Not only does Jesus show us the way to a life full of purpose, he also directs us to eternal life. Eternal life is not just a style of life, it is a quality of life. In fact, the Greek word for eternal is *aionios* which means quality.

Reading on in John 17:20-26, we see that when we believe and accept, we will know the oneness with each other and have this oneness with God and Christ. This life for God through Jesus has a rich, meaningful, and satisfying quality.

The first five verses of John 17 might be called the glory prayer. In those verses John uses a form of the word *glory* five times. Just before his cruel death on the cross, Jesus prays this prayer of glory. In his prayer Jesus begins quite naturally by addressing the Father. He simply tells God all. Jesus pours his whole soul into a prayer of adoration and thanksgiving even though he now faces death on a cross for a life devoted to glorifying God. Jesus does not come to God as an unwilling victim dragged to the altar, but as one who offers himself freely, holding back nothing, making no conditions.

Jesus chose to give himself up to death in this way, but he did it so as to bring glory to God. Through his death even a nonbeliever, a centurion, a Roman officer, could look up and say, "Truly this man was God's Son" (Mark 15:39; Matt. 27:54).

The way to give glory to God is through obedience, that is, through conforming our lives to the will of God. Christ gave perfect obedience because of his perfect love for his Father and his Father's world. What an accomplishment to be able to say, "I [have finished] the work that you gave me to do" (17:4).

God gave Christ the power to give his followers eternal life. In turn, Jesus gives glory to God by granting life to all who believe. Yet eternal life is a mystery; it is indescribable and undefined. Part of the meaning of eternal life, as we said earlier, is the quality of the life lived. It is to know God through Christ. It begins here and now. The New Testament refers to eternal life as a reality in the present as well as in the future. We can know it in this world, but it comes to its complete fullness only in the afterlife.

People in Central America know this quality of life. Having made two trips to Nicaragua to work with these courageous Christian people, I am reminded of one pleasant woman. Julia lived in the mountains near where anti-government troops had secret camps. Someone asked Julia how she and the other people coped with the fear of these Nicaraguans who raped, tortured, killed, stole, planted land mines, burned grain, kidnapped young educators, health workers, and agriculturalists. "Oh," she said, "there are times we might be afraid for a moment only. We're not a fearful people for we know the Lord is walking with us and he gives us courage and strength to face whatever comes to us." To know Jesus is to live a full life without crippling fear.

Christ, as life, also brings tension, tension between joy and sorrow. He talked of the abundant life and joy on his way to the cross, but it was at great cost for him. He sacrificed his earthly life for the fulfillment of his life in another form.

People who have been to Nicaragua come away with a blessing and a wonder at the faith of these people who have suffered so much. Like Jesus, people in oppressive situations have sacrificed life in order to gain life. They have little in the way of material goods, but they are abundantly blessed with love, generosity, forgiveness, mercy, gentleness, strength, and courage. They identify with the suffering Christ, and, more importantly, they know the hope of the resurrection. They know the joy of life in its fullest sense. These Christians can celebrate life fully.

When I was in Jalapa in 1984, our group taught the people the Virginia Reel. On the dusty streets of that northern Nicaraguan town, North Americans and Nicaraguans joyously celebrated life together.

But our Nicaraguan friends also mourn deeply. They did not, after all, choose their poverty. So we mourned with them in their personal stories about life and death. Someone told about how the contras kidnapped young people as a way of "recruiting" new troops. They nabbed two 17-year-old men, one of whom was able to escape. He found a hiding place from which he witnessed what happened to the other. After beating the young man they had taken, the contras asked him to join their group. He refused. They cut off his ears. He still refused saying he would not, could not deny his people, his country, nor his God. The group became angry; they cut out his tongue and other parts of his body. He remained strong and did not panic. The other young man marveled at his friend's calm and stamina. When he returned home, he told the mother of the tortured young man about her son's courage. She clasped her hands over her breasts and said, "I gave my son life. Now he has given me life." She had an understanding of abundant life, even in her sorrow!

In the middle of Lake Nicaragua, a large lake, are little islands called Solentináme. Ernesto Cardenál, a priest and poet, was the spiritual leader of the people who lived on the islands. After the revolution, he was called by the Sandinista government to be the Minister of Culture. But while he was still their priest he met with the people of Solentináme for Bible study and prayer. He began to record some of their sessions in a book of several volumes entitled *The Gospel of Solentináme*. In it, he recounts how the people would share what a particular passage meant to them. One session focused on God's care for the birds and for the people (Matt. 10:26-31).

> **Laureano***: I think here he's telling us not to be afraid of anything, because just as God takes care of the birds, they don't fall unless he allows it. . . . We'll fall when we have to fall or when our fall does some good, and that isn't really a fall. . . .*

> **Olivia***: As I understand it, the Gospel tells us this so we know that we're worth so much. . . . Because a person is the loveliest and most beloved creature of God. He takes care of us, and we're so valuable that even when we die we're not dead. We're just living more, and that's why we shouldn't be afraid.*

Jesus promises, "I will not leave you orphaned; I am coming to you . . . because I live, you will also live" (14:18-19). We do not have to live each day afraid of death. Eternal life is to know God.

We are assured of a future with God and Jesus, so we can face whatever comes our way, even death.

When I was younger, I didn't care for funeral services. That's not surprising because they often emphasized the pain of losing a loved one. Now most of the funeral services I attend do not just emphasize loss; they dwell on the fullness and quality of life that uplifts and renews the living, giving them a glimpse of eternity.

At a memorial service for a church choir accompanist who died, the congregation sang hymns of faith. Sometimes the people were too choked up to sing but their faith shone through their tears. The choir was finally able to sing *a capella* a moving tribute to their friend, "There'll Be Joy in the Morning."

Jesus offered abundant life saying, "You have pain now; but I will see you again, and your hearts will rejoice, and no one will take your joy from you" (John 16:22). The glory and mystery of Jesus Christ, who is life and who gives us eternal life, is all around us. When we are aware of the mystery and fully open to Jesus' gift of life, we will know complete joy. Because he lives, we also live. Hallelujah!

Discussion and Action

1. Share some times when you personally have experienced Jesus Christ as the life.
2. The author says that "the way to give glory to God is through obedience." Jesus said he glorified God by doing the work given to him (John 17:4). How do you live today in such obedience that gives glory to God?
3. Share some of your fears and anxieties about death.
4. Name some times when you felt you were "saved from death" or given a second chance for life.
5. Recall times when your faith has been strengthened at a memorial service or in spite of grief at someone's death. How do you know Jesus Christ as the life through such experiences?
6. Listen as one person reads the words of "Christ the Lord Is Risen Today," or read them in unison from your hymnals. Sing the hymn as your joyful affirmation of life in Jesus Christ.

8

Love Enacted
John 13:1-17; 21:15-17

When Jesus washed the disciples' feet, he modeled king-dom love. Then he instructed his followers to carry on the ministry of love when he told them to "feed my sheep." If we truly want to live in "the way" of Jesus, we must share love with others and let others love us too.

Personal Preparation
1. Think of a time when you were served, a time when someone did something ordinary or extraordinary for you. How did you feel? Did that make you comfortable? Or were you uncomfortable because you would rather be doing the serving? Why did you feel the way you did?
2. Read the two basic texts for this session. Then read John 13:34-35 and 15:12-14. Watch for times this week when you see such love acted out, both in person and in news stories.

Understanding
Jesus knows the cross is imminent. Yet the disciples aren't ready to take over the mission. They are slow to catch on to what Jesus tells them about the future. They think that Jesus is about to fulfill the prophecy of a Jewish political victory. In fact, two of the Synoptic Gospels (Matthew and Mark) relate the story of James and John vying for power in the new regime. Would they sit on Jesus'

right and left in his glory? The other ten disciples were incensed. How discouraged Jesus must have been, watching his beloved, misguided band of followers. But Jesus also loved his Father and was obedient. His Father said that this was the time, even though it seemed the disciples were far from ready to take over the mission.

Just before the Passover, the time of remembering, Jesus ate at the table with his friends. During the meal he arose and wrapped a towel around his waist, which must certainly have gotten the disciples' attention. Imagine the suspense! What in the world was Jesus doing?

In many countries in the world, including ancient Palestine, people with education, and certainly leaders, do not perform menial tasks. For example, a family in the United States with three daughters welcomed a young white South African exchange student into their home. The second night after he arrived, he was sitting comfortably in a chair and ordered one of the daughters to bring him a glass of water. The independent daughter, who was also sitting comfortably, looked at him and said, "You're able-bodied. Get it yourself." Clearly, the young man had to make some early adjustments.

In my own home, a Romanian refugee who stayed with us held strong opinions about men and menial tasks. One time when I had planned to be gone for a day, I prepared some food so that all he had to do was remove the pan from the refrigerator and turn on the stove; yet he preferred to use the little money he had to eat out. Romanian men did not cook. And in China the people thought it strange to see my husband, a teacher with master's degrees, very ably build things with his hands. Their reverence for position could hardly imagine this!

Respecting Jesus' position among them, the disciples could not imagine Jesus doing the menial task of pouring water and kneeling to wash and dry their feet as a mere servant. Jesus' action embarrassed them. No wonder Peter protested when Jesus kneeled to wash his feet. But through this physical act, the disciples later began to understand that Jesus was acting out love in the most concrete way possible.

Jesus' demonstration of love models the kind of love that allows us to be vulnerable to others, to let others serve and love us. Like Peter, we, too, like to be in control. We're afraid to be vulnerable even when humility and selflessness is an admired quality in people.

The Rev. William Skudlarek interviewed Brazilian Archbishop Dom Helder Camara for an article in *Sojourners* (April 1991). In the interview Dom Helder said he was "afraid of becoming proud of his humility." Once, he reported, he and Mother Teresa of Calcutta, India, were to be interviewed on television:

> *When I arrived at the studios, Mother Teresa was already there. She said, "Oh, Dom Helder, I remember how beautifully you described the way you protect yourself when you enter an auditorium filled with people who are giving you a standing ovation. I remember how you pray, 'Lord Jesus, this is your triumphal entry into Jerusalem, I'll be your little donkey.' That has really helped me. But, you know, I don't have the courage to call myself Jesus' little donkey." And then she remembered that in India, where she works, the cow is a sacred animal. "What I pray," she said, "is let me be your old cow."*

True love is being willing, like Jesus, to make yourself vulnerable, to let go of power and prestige. Jesus, knowing of Judas' terrible intent, continued to reach out to him in love. He made himself vulnerable to Judas' imminent betrayal. We can be vulnerable to those around us and to those in our world when we have the strength of knowing we belong to God. Jesus knew he came from God and would return to God. He knew his oneness with the Father. He did not kneel in weakness and in fear, but in strength and confidence.

It is said that some churches have an identity problem; they lack the confidence of knowing they are God's. In his book *Living Toward a Vision*, biblical scholar Walter Brueggemann writes:

> *The Church cannot forever live with anxiety about its own identity. It must make up its mind; and when it does, it can be yielding and receiving and vulnerable. The same resolution opens us to the Spirit and brings us to the feet of our brothers and sisters. And until those issues are settled, we are neither empowered and guided by the Spirit nor authentically vulnerable before the others. . . . He left us—kneeling and vulnerable. But he also left us free and not in doubt.*

When we know our identity as children of God, we can hear and understand more clearly Jesus' words when he said, "Feed my lambs ... tend my sheep. ... " Jesus expected that we would be strong enough to act out love as he did. What are we doing today to feed our lambs? When our days are finished here and we meet God, we won't be asked how many committees we worked on, but did we feed the sheep? Did we love and care for the poor, the prisoner, and the oppressed?

In our culture today, we are rarely confident enough in our faith to become vulnerable, to let God lead our lives. We arrogantly believe that we know best, we can do it best. We do not leave anything to chance, much less to God. I can think, however, of mission work in foreign lands that was done in humble service without concern for recognition or even success. Missionaries loved and respected the people and the countries they served. They knew their identity and that they belonged to God.

Once I heard a Nigerian speaker at an Ohio pastor's conference. He talked critically about missionaries who brought money and western ways to his homeland—western ways that became more important than the message of Jesus Christ. I wondered whether he thought all missionaries were that way. In a conversation afterwards, he remembered a group of missionaries that was quite different. "They respected us. We respected them. They gave us dignity. Yes, we learned a lot about Jesus from them."

We have a Lord to proclaim! We have an identity in which to rejoice. We are God's people. We come from God and will return to God. We are Christ's incarnate on this earth. We have so much to give. We also have so much to learn. We learn as we love and as we open ourselves to the love of others around the world who enact love.

Gilberto Aguirre, a physics professor in Nicaragua, witnessed to his realization that he belonged to God. In 1972 Aguirre was making a good salary, which enabled his family to live very comfortably. That year they welcomed a baby daughter into a family of two sons. The day after they proudly took the baby home from the hospital an earthquake hit Managua, leveling the hospital. Aguirre was so thankful his wife and daughter were safe, he repaid his good fortune by helping in the aftermath wherever he could. Suddenly his eyes were opened to all the desperate needs. He saw how the government at that time was pocketing the reconstruction money given by other governments. Through his efforts and those of many others, CEPAD, a Protestant organization much like the National Council of Churches, was formed. It began with the specific purpose of helping the poor and the needy after the earthquake and has become a highly respected church group in Nicaragua. And since that time Aguirre has worked with CEPAD because of God's call on his life to help his people.

We saw the same confidence among the residents of a leprosarium in Ethiopia. Sister Lucy, a plain woman who radiated joy, confidence, and hope, had a great deal to do with the upbeat atmosphere. The people who had leprosy laughed and talked with each other as they quickly and beautifully embroidered or picked cotton with their stubbed fists and knuckleless fingers. Sister Lucy gave of herself to help these forgotten, feared, and isolated people become a productive part of a hospital family and then the larger society.

To love and be loved is a privilege and an honor. It is also a big responsibility. Love brings tension and often a cross. Dom Helder says when he gives to the poor he is praised for the wonderful work he does. When he works at the root causes of poverty, he is crucified. Jesus loved to the end. His love, however, put him in tension and conflict with the religious authorities who believed he was a threat to their power. They didn't want change; they didn't want to be disturbed.

This can happen to us too. Love brings promise, but it can also be a threat to some. When I went to Nicaragua, North Americans I knew thought it was exciting and brave. They wanted to hear of my experiences, but they didn't want to hear the root causes of the problems because that threatened their easy, comfortable understanding of who we are. There was a tension. It was much easier for many to go along with the current government philosophy than to try to sort out the unpleasant truth. Likewise, Jesus didn't stop with talking about love. Jesus enacted love and became such a threat that he had to be eliminated.

Love requires that we become as vulnerable as Jesus was when he washed the disciples' feet, when he went to the cross. Love leads to loving action on behalf of the people "God so loved."

Discussion and Action

1. Share some of your feelings when you participate in feet-washing services. Or if this is not part of your church's practice, share your feelings when you think about acting out love as Jesus did in John 13.

2. When you think of John 13, do you first picture yourself in Peter's place, at first needing and refusing to be washed? or in Jesus' place, kneeling to be servant for another? Which is easier for you: to be giver or receiver?

3. Share situations when you saw love enacted, acted out, this week. Name one or two concrete ways you personally want to enact God's love in the coming week.

4. How well do you think the church of today knows its identity—to be God's love enacted? Being God's love acted out in the world, how would you expect the church to respond to current events (e.g., crisis in the Middle East, weapons shipments, refugee problems, racism, poverty)?

5. Decide on one response to a current world issue that your covenant group will make. Decide how and when you will make this response.

6. Claim your identity as children of God. In turn, say to each member of the group: "_(name)_ , you are a beloved child of God. Carry God's love into the world in loving action."

7. Close by singing "Love is flowing like a river, flowing out from you and me; flowing out into the desert, setting all the captives free." (Note that these words are based on Psalm 107.)

9

"It Is Finished"
John 19:1-30

From the cross, Jesus proclaimed "It is finished." His ministry was completed; he came from the Father and would return to the Father. But the mission was far from done. Jesus commissioned his followers down to the present day to carry on. Not even death can end God's mission.

Personal Preparation
1. Read John 19:1-30, using different versions of the Bible; read it at least once each day during the week.
2. After each reading, ask yourself: What does Christ's death on the cross mean to me? Spend 10 minutes a day in personal meditation and reflection.
3. At the end of each meditation time, write out some of your thoughts and feelings that help you answer the question, and take your writing to the group.

Understanding
In the end of John's Gospel, as in the beginning, we see Jesus' mission to glorify God even in the tragic death on the cross. In the crucifixion, we see what John has been working at all along—that Jesus is human, experiencing the same painful afflictions we experience, and divine, transcending the pain of the world. In the encounter with Pilate, Jesus is able to bear the humiliation with quiet

strength because he knows his identity. He comes from the Father and is going back to the Father.

Because Jesus was from God and of God, people many times discount the physical pain and torture on the cross, believing that Jesus had the power to block it out. John's account of the crucifixion does not dwell on the gruesome death of Jesus or recount the despairing cry "My God, my God, why have you forsaken me?" (see Matthew and Luke).

Yet John does recount how, in the midst of the suffering, Jesus cares for the last details of his mission. He transcends his pain to see his mother's anguish and commends her to John's care and keeping. Things have come full circle and now the Son, who was sent forth by the Father, is sending forth the mother. Moreover, the new son who stands at the foot of the cross receives the mother as his own. Together they represent the beginning of the church and the renewal of Jesus' mission.

In John's Gospel, perhaps the most important words from the cross are "It is finished." Here these words do not mean that Jesus' mission has ended or that it has failed. His words mean that what he came to do is fulfilled. To complete the mission Jesus gives over his spirit and returns to God. Jesus' agony does not weaken his divinity; it enhances his humanity, his courage, his commitment, his love of God.

Jesus felt a oneness, a completeness, and fulfillment with the Father all through his life and also in his death. He didn't need to shout it out. It was a quiet knowing and assurance. At one time I had a serious bout in the hospital that left me weak and vulnerable. My husband was there with me, willing to do whatever I needed. We had been married 44 years. There was no need for him to shout at me, "I'm here." In my drowsy, weakened state, I just knew and felt his presence—a quiet assurance. When any one of us has walked with the Lord for many years, we, too, find that quiet assurance—that strength that helps us through difficult times.

Jesus came from God with a mission to tell people of God's love. It is a message of grace. All people should know joy and peace because they recognize and accept God's grace and fellowship with each other. What a simple message and yet how complex and difficult in our world of intrigue, self-centeredness, and greed.

Jesus, loving and caring for all people, became a threat to the status quo, and they finally crucified him. Yet, in spite of the odds, he fulfilled his mission, even to the very end, to the humiliating, painful, crucified end. He could say with conviction, "It is finished." This cry was not the wearied cry of defeat; but it was one of triumph. The victory was won.

While his mission was accomplished on that day 2000 years ago, it was the beginning of a mission that goes on today. It is up to each of us to decide what to do with that mission.

Throughout history, from the first disciples to the present age, people at the forefront of the struggle to rectify injustice have been killed for their loyalty to God's mission, God's justice.

When Oscar Romero was named Archbishop of El Salvador, he was a person of compromise, a patient priest who did not believe in "making waves." But he couldn't avoid seeing the grave injustices being perpetrated on the poor by the rich aristocracy. He came to believe that "economic injustice is the root cause of our problems. From it stems all the violence." He became immersed in trying to right these injustices. On March 24, 1980, three years after becoming Archbishop, Oscar Romero was killed while he was giving communion to his people. Just days before his assassination he said, "I have been threatened with death. If they kill me, I will arise in the Salvadoran people. Let my blood be a seed of freedom and the sign that hope will soon be reality. A bishop will die, but the Church of God, which is the people, will never perish."

Much of the popular religion of our day leads people to believe that if they live a good life, they'll be prosperous, popular, and successful. Too many people have bought into this fashionable religion found in fashionable places among fashionable people; but this is not biblical religion. It is not Christ's way. The biblical way is not one that prizes a certain level of comfort. The biblical way is one of struggle and triumph.

Someone told of seeing a butterfly start to emerge from its chrysalis and, hating to see the way it was struggling, began to help it. However, in taking over and helping it bypass the agonizing struggle, this "help" actually crippled the butterfly. Its wings didn't develop enough to lift it into the air. It was not allowed to accomplish its work.

"It is finished" is a cry of true triumph. But even though God triumphed ultimately in the resurrection, we still find there are many failures in our world. We all too often feel as though "it" is finished—our lives, our careers, our missions. Why can't our faith make a difference in our own war-torn, crime-ridden nation? Our world is not as safe in 1991 as it was in 1981. Failures abound. Nevertheless, even in rat-infested housing projects; on city streets where youths cut each other down over petty arguments and imagined slights; in the narrow streets of old Jerusalem, with tense, trigger-ready Israeli soldiers and masked Palestinian boys throwing rocks, there are still hearts that are ruled by love.

We are touched and uplifted by stories of renewal and resurrection. The story was told of a little three-year-old Palestinian girl who, sitting in a street of Old Jerusalem, had picked up a stone. An Israeli soldier was heading for her. The adults around were petrified, for usually Israeli soldiers arrested anyone with stones regardless of their age. The soldier went up to the little girl, picked her up, talked with her, and hugged her. Then he took the stone, set her down again, and walked away.

Resurrection is happening in our hemisphere, too. Thousands from our country have gone into Nicaragua to learn of the people's struggle and to work side-by-side with them. The Church of the Saviour in Washington, D.C., is one group that sponsored a trip for Americans who wanted to meet and work with the Nicaraguans. A very wealthy woman and a woman on welfare went from their church. They were assigned to be roommates for the two-week experience. They not only learned about Nicaragua, they also learned about each other. For them it was a breakthrough, a resurrection of Jesus' mission.

While fashionable religion is found in the "right" places, Christ's way often leads to the "wrong" places, into the dark streets where the masses of humankind live with the "down and outers." Jesus was concerned about reaching out to people such as these, both the fashionable and the unfashionable, with his message of love. But since Jesus is gone and his mission finished, what are we to do? The message of John's Gospel tells us that we must receive the mission from the cross, making it our own.

In the pain and suffering of our day, the crucified God is planted in the midst of crucified men and women. We still can capture the glory and mystery of faith when we glorify God with our love. The mission makes us realize anew, "God is with us."

Discussion and Action

1. Share your notes about the meaning of Christ's death for you.

2. Discuss how John's Gospel shows Jesus' mission finished, yet going on. Do you agree with the author that Jesus' statements to his mother and the disciple he loved at the foot of his cross represent his mission continuing?

3. Share times when joy has come out of suffering and pain, when you have known victory coming out of defeat.

4. Name people throughout history who have been persecuted, tortured, killed for their faith. How have they been part of Christ's victory?

5. Share simple stories from life today (such as the soldier and the child with a stone) that symbolize renewal and resurrection.

6. Close with sentence prayers, thanking God for the life, death, and resurrection of Jesus Christ, for resurrection times we know today, and for calling us to mission in the world.

10

The Promise
John 14:15-21; 20:19-22

Though Jesus fulfilled his mission and left the world, he did not abandon it. In his place, Jesus promised an Advocate, the Holy Spirit that dwells with us. Nor did our faith leave us when Jesus died on the cross. Real faith grows and deepens under the care and presence of the Holy Spirit.

Personal Preparation
1. Read the scriptures for this session. Then look up other scriptures that give different names, characteristics, and activities of the Holy Spirit.
2. Make a list of these names and characteristics of the Spirit; take it to your group meeting.
3. Recall specific times when you have known the Holy Spirit present in your life.

Understanding
The glory and mystery of which John writes are endless. We can never fully know the answers to the eternal questions. But Christ does not want his disciples or his later followers to stop with knowing about Jesus. We're to go beyond Jesus, to keep growing and learning through the Holy Spirit who comes from God and who John calls our "Advocate" (14:16). To feel we know it all because we know about Jesus who lived 2000 years ago is to miss a

fundamental part of Christ's teachings and to miss his promise. If we think we know it all, we fail to see the eternal work of God in our midst through the Holy Spirit.

The vastness of God is like an ocean. Some people may stand at the edge of the water and believe they know all about the ocean because they have touched it. Yet they've only touched the surface. The wideness, the depth, the mystery, and the wonder of the ocean has much more to be revealed: life teeming within it, more tides, mountains, canyons, and reefs than can be observed from the shore.

So it is with Jesus the Christ. Some Christians stop with just knowing Jesus. Some feel that to believe there could be anything more than Jesus is wrong. But he, in the form of the Advocate or Holy Spirit, keeps revealing the glory of God. We are not meant to remain babes in Christ; we are meant to grow up in Christ.

When I look back at my own life, I remember a time in my husband's first pastorate when we had no money to go to the denomination's annual meeting and the congregation had no money to send us. Since childhood I had gone almost every year to this important gathering of the church, and it had become very important to me. How well I remember the self-pity and sadness about not going that one year. In spite of that disappointment, we remained open to God's leading. Since those years we have traveled in all but four of the states and have lived or traveled in fifteen countries. Life under God's guidance has enabled us to meet a wide variety of people and work in many different geographical locations we would never have dreamed of.

At the fulfillment of his mission, Jesus prepared the new family of God to carry on his mission. The cross was not by any means the end of God's presence with us. Jesus promised that even as God had sent Jesus, so God would send the Holy Spirit. John's special term for the Holy Spirit is Advocate, someone who comes on our behalf to speak for us, to represent us.

The Spirit always presents the truth. According to John, the Spirit is our teacher and helper. When life becomes overwhelming or almost unbearable, we find the Spirit is with us to give us strength and courage and we do not break. The Spirit counsels and guides.

The Holy Spirit in John's Gospel is also called the Comforter and the Counselor and the Paraclete. These names remind us of God's care for us and assure us that we were not abandoned when Jesus left the world.

The promise of the Holy Spirit is available to each of us. But too often we ignore that promise or are afraid to trust it. Our own wants and desires creep in where trust and obedience should be, and then we get way off base. The Advocate must guide us back to the mission that Christ left us. Spirit-rooted friends and the church can help keep us focused in the right direction.

In Acts 2 Luke gives us a different picture of the Spirit—an outward, lively Spirit, a mighty wind, tongues of fire and voices speaking in other tongues. John's and Luke's descriptions of the Holy Spirit do not, however, contradict each other. They enlarge our understanding of who God is. God doesn't operate just one way. Christendom is sometimes divided because we fail to recognize this fact.

In our personal lives we find the Spirit meets our different needs. There are times I want to be still and find the quiet, assuring guidance of the Spirit. At other times I want to walk and listen to the Spirit in God's creation all around—the laughing brook, the chattering birds, the wind sighing in the trees. At other times I want to look at the blue sky and lift my thoughts above to learn and envision more of God's wisdom and plan for the world. There are other times I want to be with people. At times I want to sing joyously and lift my arms in praise and cry, "Thank you, thank you, God!" Again there are times I am moved to cry at the pain of another or I am moved to serve another person humbly or to receive another's ministry.

We can rejoice with each other as we obey the various calls of the Holy Spirit. The Spirit also gives us the ability to discern and at times the power to keep still and say nothing. At other times, the Spirit gives us the courage to speak up and share important concerns.

Immediately after he talks about the Advocate, Jesus says, "Peace I leave with you . . . " (14:25-26). This is peace, not as the world gives, but an inner peace, a peace that those in the world cannot understand. We don't need to be afraid of the Spirit or the times in which we live. When we accept and embrace the Spirit, we are able to cope with our world.

For ten years I was a supervisor in the welfare department. During one particular period, morale among the workers was at an all-time low. There was dissatisfaction with management and some very hostile feelings within the department. I prayed daily, as I walked to work, that any negatives that hit me could be transformed to feelings of love. One morning, some workers came into my office just to sit (this was unusual for there was never time to do that), and later other workers came into my office just to sit. Around noon that same day several others, including supervisors, came in. Then someone explained, "It is so peaceful here—an oasis. How do you do it?"

Peace in the midst of turmoil. That is the gift of the Holy Spirit. A prize was once awarded for the best picture depicting peace. There were many beautiful pastoral scenes and other peaceful paintings. But the one that won the prize showed a rocky cliff with rain beating down and angry waves pummeling the coast. High on the cliff, in a crevice, a dove was sitting on her nest. Like the dove, we can know peace in everyday life even though storms are raging around us.

The disciples were a scared and defeated group. They had let Jesus down; they also felt Jesus had let them down; the religious leaders were after them; their dreams were shattered; their leader was disgraced; their future had gone down the drain. How they had failed! But in the midst of their despair, Jesus came to them with "Peace be with you" (20:19). Peace! Jesus offered peace that comes from deep within when one knows the Lord.

Jesus was saying to the disciples that, despite his departure, they could rely on him. No matter if they despaired and doubted, Jesus still loved them. Jesus and God were still trusting them with the mission. "As the Father has sent me, so I send you" (20:21). It is something to entrust someone with an important mission when they have proven trustworthy; but to entrust the saving of the world to this band of fearful, despairing, doubting, denying disciples depicts both the glory and the mystery of God's way.

Jesus, by entrusting the disciples again with the mission, breathed new life into them; he gave them something now he had not been able to give before. Why? Perhaps they were more humble, more open to receive. Perhaps they had been too arrogant, too self-assured, too confident. But now, having learned from their frightening experiences, they realized they were not able to go it alone. They needed to receive all that Christ could give them. They needed the Holy Spirit for themselves, but they also needed the Spirit to empower them to carry out the mission. And what a band of courageous, strong, forceful, articulate followers these disciples became!

The promise that comes to us today is as relevant as it was for the disciples. If we attempt to live life out of our own strength and with our own plans, we are doomed to despair and ineffectiveness.

The disciples of any age draw on the strength of the Holy Spirit, which they do not have in themselves. These times, especially, call for Spirit-empowered lives to carry out the mission of Christ.

When the church is filled with the Spirit, wonders occur. One psychiatrist said more healing takes place in the Sunday morning worship service than we can know. But by the same token the church has often failed. My husband says of its mistakes, "The church stumbles forward." Yet, when we look back, it is amazing how the church has found its way through difficulties that seemed insurmountable and problems that apparently could not be solved. The Spirit moves when we are open and ready to receive.

His promise comes to us today. God's creation is good. Christ promises a life of abundant living and joy. Jesus came with the good news that God is a God of love, that God loves us. Jesus promised that we would not be alone in this life. The Spirit walks with us leading us to fulfillment and joy. A new day is emerging. Hallelujah! Amen!

Discussion and Action

1. Look at the list that you have made about the Holy Spirit. Perhaps you will want to combine your lists into one list to have in front of the group during this final study time.
2. Share some of the important things you have learned from this study of John's Gospel about the mystery and the glory of God as revealed through the Son, Jesus Christ.
3. Share times in your life when you were led or supported or enabled or called out by the Holy Spirit.
4. Think of the worst scenario of turmoil in your present life. What would it take to know the peace of God in the midst of such turmoil? Write down your thoughts and then share them with the group.
5. Name ways you have seen the Holy Spirit working with people in your covenant group, in the congregation, and in the world in the past three months.
6. Close by singing favorite hymns about the mystery and the glory of God's presence with us today, through the Holy Spirit. Possibilities include: "Breathe upon Us, Holy Spirit," "Move in Our Midst, Thou Spirit of God," "Gracious Spirit, Dwell with Me," "Spirit of the Living God."

Suggestions for Sharing and Prayer

This material is designed for covenant Bible study groups that spend one hour in sharing and praying together, followed by one hour of Bible study. Some suggestions are offered here to help relate your sharing to your study of *Mystery and Glory in John's Gospel*. Session-by-session ideas are given first, followed by general resources. Use the ones you find most helpful. Also bring your own ideas for sharing and worshiping together in your covenant group. June Adams Gibble, Elgin, Illinois, compiled this guide.

1. God's Glory Revealed

❑ Begin by forming as a covenant group (see "Forming a Covenant Group" in the general resources section). Talk about covenant expectations (p. 71); use the burlap cross symbol if you choose (p. 72); share a litany (p. 72) and covenant prayer (p. 73); and learn the song "Weave" (p. 77).

❑ As you think about mystery and glory in this Gospel, share a favorite mystery story or movie. What do you like about mystery? What do you dislike about mystery?

❑ Learn and sing the hymn "I Will Sing of the Mercies of the Lord" (p. 78).

2. Dwelling Among Us

❑ Recall camping experiences, especially times when you have stayed in a tent. How do you live together in close quarters?

❑ Share times when you felt especially close to God (e.g., at church camp, at sunrise, at church).

❑ Think of a special word whose sound you like, a word that has power for you.

❑ Sing "Peace is flowing like a river, flowing out to you and me; flowing out into the desert, setting all the captives free" (also Love is . . ./Joy is . . .).

3. The World: To Love or Reject?

☐ Recall and share times when as child or youth you were not allowed to do something because it was "too worldly."

☐ Share in the American Indian ritual described in this lesson, using water to symbolize what you receive from God. Share what you learned with others (use a People of the Covenant mug if you have one).

> Face west, and pray for openness to whatever God has for you this day; take a drink, symbolizing your act of receiving openness.
>
> Face north, and pray for wisdom; again, take a drink, symbolizing your act of receiving wisdom.
>
> Face east, and pray for new insights and ideas; again, drink, symbolizing your act of receiving new insights.
>
> Face south, and pray for more trust in God; drink, symbolizing your act of trusting God.

☐ Acknowledge one at a time that each of you has received these things, with the first speaker holding the cup and then passing it off to the next person.

☐ Sing "He's Got the Whole World in His Hands," adding phrases of your own that speak of people, groups, and actions in today's world (e.g., the poor and the homeless, the US government, our congregation, our families and friends, the church in other countries, the people of Iraq).

4. "I AM . . . "

☐ Recall some of your earliest memories of who Jesus is.

☐ Share favorite hymns that speak of who Jesus is for you (for example, "Shepherd of Tender Youth" pictures Jesus as a shepherd and a guide.) Sing some of these hymns together.

☐ Use the faith affirmation "He was the Son of God; he was the Son of man."

☐ Worship, using the symbol of Jesus giving living water. Use phrases from John 4:7-15, the litany "Give Us Living Water" (p. 73). Then pour water for each other, and drink together. You may want to use the hymn "Fill My Cup, Lord" (. . . fill my cup, fill it up, and make me whole). Use People of the Covenant mugs if you have them.

5. Jesus Christ: The Way

- ❑ Recall times when someone gave you directions and you still couldn't find the way.

- ❑ Share times when you have been a "doubting Thomas," raising doubts and questions about Jesus' way. What happened? Did your questioning bring you to deeper faith?

- ❑ View and discuss "By the Manner of Their Living" (segment 7) of the video called *Journey In Jesus' Way.* (Rent from Brethren Press, 1-800-323-8039.)

- ❑ Symbolize your willingness to help each other walk in "the way." Stand up to form a circle; begin humming the melody of "Peace is flowing like a river. . . . " While singing these words, place your hands on the shoulders of the person on your right. Then place your hands on the shoulders of the person on your left while singing the words "Love is flowing. . . . " Finally, join hands in the circle, raise them upward, and all together say, "Amen! Amen! Amen!"

6. Jesus Christ: The Truth

- ❑ Share times when as a child you were admonished to "tell the truth." Can you remember when you forgetfully or spitefully "told a lie" instead?

- ❑ Use hymnals to find hymns that speak about the truth you know in Jesus Christ (e.g., "Ask ye what great thing I know . . . Jesus Christ, the crucified" or "I know not why God's wondrous grace. . . . but I know whom I have believed . . . "). Sing some of your favorites.

- ❑ Come to prayer, using the words of the second stanza of "Gracious Spirit, Dwell with Me" on page 76 ("Truthful Spirit, dwell with me, I myself would truthful be. . . . ") Follow with silent prayer, then sentence prayers. Close by having one voice sing these words and the whole group join in as the verse is repeated.

7. Jesus Christ: The Life

- ❑ Bring in pictures that speak to you of life—full life, life over-flowing with goodness, with abundance. Spend sharing time talking about abundance in your life, putting the pictures on construction paper and making a scrapbook or a large poster/collage. Include the words from John 10:10 (or a paraphrase) with your work. Decide how you will share this with others.

❑ View "Stewards of God's Gifts" (segment 11) or "Responding to God's Grace" (segment 12) of the video *Journey in Jesus' Way.*

❑ Use the hymn "Ask Ye What Great Thing I Know" as a prayer. One person could read the words and sing one or two stanzas. The group could sing stanzas 3 and 4 after they are read; then hum the melody once or twice as the closing moments of prayer.

8. Love Enacted

❑ Share times you remember from childhood when someone gave love to you through an action. Then name times in the past year when someone gave love through an unexpected action.

❑ Look at words of the hymn "Love Divine, All Loves Excelling," especially these:

> *Love divine, all loves excelling,*
> *Joy of heaven, to earth come down . . .*
> *Jesus, thou art all compassion*
> *Pure, unbounded love thou art . . .*
> *Read the words, sing them, feel them in your heart and*
> *in your life.*

❑ Share other hymns that speak of love enacted (e.g., "Jesu, Jesu, Fill Us with Your Love").

❑ Plan a feetwashing service for your group, using the John 13:1-17 text.

9. "It Is Finished"

❑ Tell about a time you completed a major project or job or goal (such as schooling) in the past year. How do you feel when you finish something?

❑ Have you shared experiences or started projects during your covenant group meeting time that need some follow-up?

Check with people in the group to find out how a shared situation in their life is going.

❏ Sing some of the hymns about Christ's death that are important for you.

❏ Pray for each person in your group by name, perhaps going around the circle; or everyone offer sentence prayers for each person.

10. The Promise

❏ Sing "Peace is flowing like a river, flowing out *to* you and me . . . . " Repeat, using "God's love . . . " and then "God's peace . . . . " Sing this again, using the word *from* each time, symbolizing that God's peace and love are given to us and then we share his peace and love with others.

❏ Share with each person: "I see God's Spirit working in your life in these ways: _____. " Follow the sharing with prayers for each person; and then sing "Gracious Spirit, Dwell with Me" (p. 76).

❏ Give each member of the group a People of the Covenant mug. Plant flowers or green plants in them; make dried flower arrangements; or fill them with seashells or other keepsakes. This activity can be done during sharing time, or each person can take a mug home the prior week, fill it, and bring it back to give to someone.

❏ Close by singing "Weave, weave, weave us together . . . " (p. 77).

General Sharing and Prayer Resources

Forming a Covenant Group

Covenant Expectations

Covenant-making is significant throughout the biblical story. God made covenants with Noah, Abraham, and Moses. Jeremiah speaks about God making a covenant with the people, "written on the heart." In the New Testament, Jesus is identified as the mediator of the new covenant, and the early believers lived out of covenant relationships. Throughout history people have lived in covenant relationship with God and within community.

Christians today also covenant with God and make commitments with each other. Such covenants help believers to live out their faith. God's empowerment comes to them as they gather in covenant community to pray and study, share and receive, reflect and act.

People of the Covenant is a program that is anchored in this covenantal history of God's people. It is a network of covenantal relationships. Denominations, districts or regions, congregations, small groups, and individuals all make covenants. Covenant group members commit themselves to the mission statement, seeking "to become more:

- biblically informed so they better understand the revelation of God;

- globally aware so they know themselves better connected with all of God's world;

- relationally sensitive to God, self, and others."

The Burlap Cross Symbol

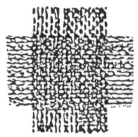

The imperfections of the burlap cross, its rough texture and unrefined fabric, the interweaving of threads, the uniqueness of each strand, are elements which are present within the covenant group. The people in the groups are imperfect, unpolished, interrelated with each other, yet still unique beings.

The shape that this collection of imperfect threads creates is the cross, symbolizing for all Christians the resurrection and presence of Christ our Savior. A covenant group is something akin to this burlap cross. It unites common, ordinary people and sends them out again in all directions to be in the world.

A Litany of Commitment

All: We are a people of the covenant;
                Out of our commitment to Christ,
                    we seek to become:

Group1:   more biblically informed
                    so we understand better God's revelation;

Group 2:   more globally aware
                    so we know ourselves connected with all of God's people;

Group 1:   more relationally sensitive to God, self, and others.

All: We are a people of the covenant;
                We promise:

Group 2:   to seek ways of living out and sharing our faith;

Group 1:   to participate actively in congregational life;

Group 2:   to be open to the leading of the Spirit in our lives.

All: We are a people of the covenant;
                We commit ourselves:

Group 1:   to attend each group meeting, so far as possible;

Group 2:   to prepare through Bible study, prayer, and action;

Group 1:   to share thoughts and feelings, as appropriate;

Group 2:   to encourage each other on our faith journeys.

All: We are a people of the covenant.
> [The preceding information and Litany of Commitment are from the People of the Covenant program, Church of the Brethren General Board, 1451 Dundee Avenue, Elgin, Illinois 60120.]

A Covenant Prayer

O God, we renew the covenant.
Spoken by our fathers and mothers,
   sung in homes and meeting houses,
      written by the pens of pilgrims and preachers.
This covenant we know is costly;
   but there is nothing of greater value.
So we accept your gifts and promises
   with thanksgiving;
And offer you our lives and our love. Amen.
> By Leland Wilson. Adapted from *The Gifts We Bring*, Vol. 2
> (Worship Resources for Stewardship and Mission).

A Litany: Give Us Living Water

Give us living water
   So that we never thirst again.
Let us treat each other as sisters and brothers in Christ
   So that we never thirst again.
Let us know God's gift
   So that we can share your salvation.
Give us the water of life
   So that we can share it with those who thirst.
Give us water from the fountain,
   Water for eternal life.
Grant us life in your Spirit
   So that we can be truly free.
Speak with us, Jesus,
   So that we know your truth.
Thank you, God,
   for you are the fresh water of eternal life. Amen.
> By Olga Serrano, from *Women at the Well*.
> Copyright 1987, Womaen's Caucus,
> Church of the Brethren.
> Used by permission.

Litany: He Was the Son of God ... Son of Man

He was the Son of God.
> He was the Son of man.

He came down from heaven.
> He was born in a stable.

Kings came to his cradle.
> His first home was a cave.

He was born to be a king.
> He was a child of Mary.

He was the greatest among rulers.
> He was the least among servants.

He was loved and honored.
> He was despised and rejected.

He was gentle and loving.
> He made many enemies.

He counseled Perfection.
> He was a friend of sinners.

He was a joyful companion.
> He was a man of sorrows.

He said, "Rejoice."
> He said, "Repent."

"Love God with all your heart."
> "Love your neighbor as yourself."

"Don't be anxious."
> "Count the cost."

"Deny yourself."
> "Ask and receive."

In him was life.
> He died on the cross.

He was a historic person.
> He lives today.

He was Jesus of Nazareth.
> He is Christ the Lord.

By Kenneth Morse. From *We Gather Together:*
Worship Resources for the Church of the Brethren,
Copyright 1979, Brethren Press.
Used by permission.

Hymns To Use
(for singing and using words as prayer or litany)

"I Will Sing of the Mercies of the Lord"

"I Know Not Why God's Wondrous Grace"

"Gracious Spirit, Dwell with Me"

"Breathe On Me, Breath of God"

"O God, in Restless Living"

"Ask Ye What Great Thing I Know"

"Come Let Us All Unite"

I've got peace like a river . . . in my soul.
I've got joy like a fountain . . . in my soul.
I've got love like an ocean . . . in my soul.

Call to Worship

We are called to open our hearts to the Holy Spirit
   that God's love may be poured in.
We are called to open our hearts to faith
   that the love of Christ may dwell within.
We are promised that when we respond to this call,
   we will be filled with all the fullness of God.
We come to worship God.

By Norm Esdon, taken from *A New Heart and a New Spirit*.
Copyright 1992, Ecumenical Center for
Stewardship Studies, Indianapolis, Indiana.
Used with permission.

Gracious Spirit, Dwell with Me

Thomas T. Lynch, 1855, alt.

Richard Redhead, 1853

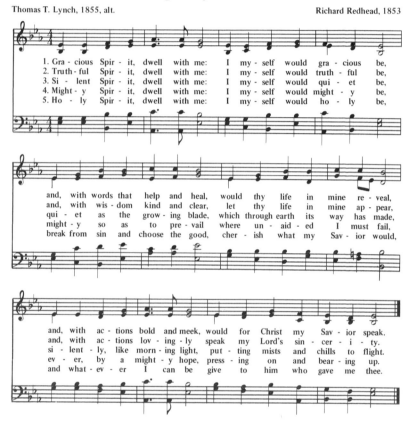

1. Gra - cious Spir - it, dwell with me: I my - self would gra - cious be,
2. Truth - ful Spir - it, dwell with me: I my - self would truth - ful be,
3. Si - lent Spir - it, dwell with me: I my - self would qui - et be,
4. Might - y Spir - it, dwell with me: I my - self would might - y be,
5. Ho - ly Spir - it, dwell with me: I my - self would ho - ly be,

and, with words that help and heal, would thy life in mine re - veal,
and, with wis - dom kind and clear, let thy life in mine ap - pear,
qui - et as the grow - ing blade, which through earth its way has made,
might - y so as to pre - vail where un - aid - ed I must fail,
break from sin and choose the good, cher - ish what my Sav - ior would,

and, with ac - tions bold and meek, would for Christ my Sav - ior speak.
and, with ac - tions lov - ing - ly speak my Lord's sin - cer - i - ty.
si - lent - ly, like morn - ing light, put - ting mists and chills to flight.
ev - er, by a might - y hope, press - ing on and bear - ing up.
and what - ev - er I can be give to him who gave me thee.

Weave

Rosemary Crow

Refrain

Weave, weave, weave us to-geth-er. Weave us to-geth-er in
u-ni-ty and love. _____ Weave, weave, weave us to-geth-er,
Weave us to-geth-er, to-geth-er in love. _____ 3. (A)

1. We are ma-ny tex - tures, we are ma-ny col - ors,
2. We are dif-f'rent in - stru-ments play-ing our own mel - o - dies
3. Mo - ment a - go we did not know our

each one dif-f'rent from the oth - er. _____ But
each one tun-ing to a dif-f'rent key. _____ But
u - ni - ty, on - ly di - ver - si - ty. _____ Now the

we are en-twined with one an - oth - er in one great tap - es - try.
we are all play - ing in har - mo - ny in one great sym- pho - ny.
Christ in me greets the Christ in thee in one great fam - i - ly.

I Will Sing of the Mercies

Psalm 89:1   Traditional

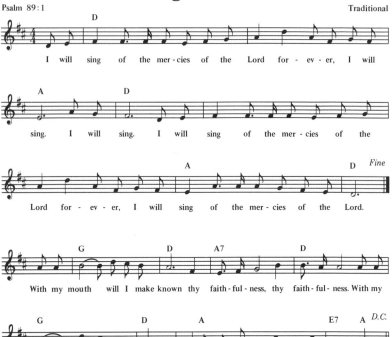

Other Covenant Bible Studies available from *faithQuest*: